INVADING COLOMBIA

Guatemala Bay

Rio Hacha
Sta Marta
Coro
Maracaibo
Cartagena
B. v. Darien
Mompoz
Gibraltar
Merida
Concep
caragua
See
S. Juan
Jose
Panama
Antioquia
Cauca
Medellin
Socorro
Meta
Varinas
Pamplona
Apu

I. Quibo
Mariato Sp.
Busen von Panama
Quibdo
Tunja
Pore
Tomo
Ottomaken

Buenaventura
Honda
Bogota
Neyva
Guaviare
F. S. Ag

Magdalene

Popayan
F. S. Ag
Meridan

Guascama Sp.
Pasto
F. S.
Gabriel

C. S. Francisco
Ibarra
1
Caqueta od.

Quito
Napo
St Miguel
Mana

Puerto Viega
Chimboeasso
Columba
Maynas
I. Jça Parana

Guayaqui
Cuenca
Maranno
Olivenc

I. Puna
St Fernando

S. Regis de los
Carapuch

Loxa
Yameos

Paita
Jaen de Bracamoros
Sarayacu
Veuschte

Sechara

Aguja Sp.

GROSS

ECU

GRANADA

DORADO

Mavorunas Ind.

INVADING COLOMBIA

Spanish Accounts of the
Gonzalo Jiménez de Quesada Expedition of Conquest

J. Michael Francis

The Pennsylvania State University Press
University Park, Pennsylvania

Library of Congress Cataloging-in-Publication Data

Invading Colombia : Spanish accounts of the Gonzalo
Jimenez de Quesada expedition of conquest / J. Michael
Francis [compilador].
    p.   cm.—(Latin American originals ; 1)
Includes bibliographical references and index.
ISBN-13: 978-0-271-02936-8 (pbk. : alk. paper)
1. Colombia—Discovery and exploration—Spanish.
2. Colombia—History–To 1810—Sources.
3. JimÈnez de Quesada, Gonzalo, d. 1579.
I. Francis, J. Michael (John Michael).

F2272.I58 2007
986.1—dc22
2007033481

CONTENTS

MAPS AND TABLES

This volume, LAO 1, *Invading Colombia,* along with LAO 2, *Invading Guatemala,* launch a new series of primary source texts on colonial and nineteenth-century Latin America. Latin American Originals (LAO) presents accessible, affordable editions of texts translated into English—often for the very first time. Some of the source texts were published in the colonial period in their original language (Spanish, Portuguese, or Latin), while others are archival documents written in Spanish or Portuguese or in indigenous languages such as Nahuatl, Zapotec, and Maya. The contributing authors are historians, anthropologists, art historians, and scholars of literature; they have developed a specialized knowledge that allows them to locate, translate, and present these texts in a way that contributes to scholars' understanding of the period, while also making them readable for students and nonspecialists.

J. Michael Francis is one such author. He received his doctorate from the University of Cambridge in 1998 and has since taught Latin American history at the University of North Florida, where he is an associate professor, while continuing to study and publish on the history of the sixteenth-century New Kingdom of Granada (today's Colombia). In the course of doing research in the Spanish imperial archives in Seville, Francis uncovered a treasure trove of documents written by Spaniards who had survived their invasion of Colombia in the 1530s. These sources allowed him to construct a narrative of the invasion told by multiple witnesses. Almost none of the documents have been published before, and none have ever been published in English.

If that fact alone does not make this volume a major—and fascinating—contribution to the history of conquest and colonization in the Americas, two other aspects of the story are equally striking. First, the early part of the narrative eerily echoes the story of Francisco Pizarro's invasion of the Inca Empire just a few years before; and yet, second, that tale is famous, and this one almost completely unknown. Why this vast discrepancy? And which invasion was more typical of the Spanish experiences of the era? Why did the young lawyer-conquistador Gonzalo Jiménez de Quesada, who led more Spaniards into Colombia than Hernando Cortés led into Mexico or Pizarro into Peru, fail to go down in the history books alongside those two legendary compatriots of his? Is it possible that the well-known invasions that brought down empires tell us less about the Spanish Conquest—and are in the end less interesting— than disastrous invasions such as Jiménez de Quesada's? I think the answer may be yes, and I invite the reader to ponder the question as the narrative presented below unfolds in all its glorious, grim detail.

—Matthew Restall

A great many soldiers walked barefoot, blood spilling from

the open wounds on their feet; and many died from hunger

because we found few settlements from which to gather

enough provisions for such a large group. And thus the men

died, ten at a time; others simply were left behind [to die]

along the way. Still others, while resting in their hammocks,

were snatched by tigers. And some soldiers who ventured

down to the Río Grande to gather [water], were ripped to

pieces and eaten by caimans, while the [other] soldiers [stood

by], helpless to save them.

The storyline follows a familiar plot.[1] It is the third decade of the sixteenth century, and a small band of Spanish adventurers, fewer than two hundred in all, climb the western flank of the South American Andes. They have timed their arrival well; the local indigenous population is divided, engaged in a bitter civil war between two rival factions. The conflict not only allows the Spaniards to exploit these deep political divisions, it also prevents any unified defense against the newcomers, who quickly plot their strategy. In accordance with long-established military procedure in the Americas, the Spaniards seize the powerful ruler and place him under house arrest. To secure his safe release, the captive leader makes a tantalizing offer. In exchange for his freedom, he offers to fill an entire room with a treasure of precious metals and gemstones. The Spaniards accept. To this point in the story, despite the overwhelming numerical superiority of indigenous forces, not a single Spaniard has lost his life in combat. The native ruler is not so fortunate.

Despite the obvious similarities, the preceding paragraph does not describe the opening phase of the Spanish conquest of Peru.[2] And the setting for this story is not the northern Andean city of Cajamarca, famous site of Francisco Pizarro's 1532 encounter with the Inca ruler Atahualpa. Instead, the passage chronicles a series of events that began to unfold roughly four years later and more than six hundred

1. The first epigraph comes from servicios y méritos de Juan Ramírez de Hinojosa, AGI Patronato 160, N. 3, R. 1, fol. 310v. At least one member of Jiménez's expedition, Juan Lorenzo, was killed by a cayman; another Spaniard, a man by the name of Juan Serrano, was said to have been pulled from his hammock and eaten by a "tiger." See José Ignacio Avellaneda Navas, *La expedición de Gonzalo Jiménez de Quesada al Mar del Sur y la creación del Nuevo Reino de Granada* (Bogotá: Banco de la República, 1995), 22–23.

2. To date, the most accessible narrative account of the conquest of Peru remains John Hemming, *The Conquest of the Incas* (London: Macmillan, 1970).

miles north of Cajamarca, in a region that would later become the New Kingdom of Granada (modern Colombia).[3]

In early April 1536, a twenty-seven-year-old lawyer named Gonzalo Jiménez de Quesada led a military expedition from the coastal city of Santa Marta deep into the interior of what is today modern Colombia. With roughly eight hundred Spaniards and an undetermined number of native carriers and black slaves, the Jiménez expedition was larger than the combined forces under Hernando Cortés in Mexico and Francisco Pizarro in Peru. Jiménez's men were divided into two separate groups, with five to six hundred Spaniards marching overland, supported by more than two hundred others who boarded five brigantines and sailed up the Magdalena River. The official purpose of the expedition was twofold: to find an overland route from Colombia's Caribbean coast to newly conquered Peru, and to follow the Magdalena River to discover its source, which some believed would lead the expedition to the South Sea (the Pacific Ocean). It found neither. Instead, nearly three-quarters of Jiménez's men perished, most from illness, hunger, and malnutrition.[4] Some Spaniards fell victim to jaguar or cayman attacks, or to mortal wounds from native arrows laced with the deadly twenty-four-hour poison. Others, too exhausted or injured to continue, limped back to the brigantines and returned to Santa Marta. Yet, despite the high casualty rate, for the 179 survivors of the twelve-month venture, the expedition proved to be one of the most profitable campaigns of the sixteenth century. In early March 1537, almost a full year after they had set out from Santa Marta, Jiménez and his men successfully crossed the Opón Mountains and reached the densely populated and fertile plains of Colombia's eastern highlands, home to the Muisca.

Jiménez and his men recognized immediately the importance of their discovery. The dense population, rich agricultural lands, pleasant climate, splendid public architecture, and, perhaps most important,

3. Although the conquest narrative for New Granada appears to borrow directly from Pizarro's conquest of Peru, it is important to recognize that this was not unique. Similar stories were played out elsewhere in the Americas, as various Spanish expeditions followed a set of standard military procedures. For a more detailed overview of these conquest procedures, see Matthew Restall, *Seven Myths of the Spanish Conquest* (New York: Oxford University Press, 2003), 18–26.

4. For a more detailed explanation of the causes of death, see José Ignacio Avellaneda Navas, *The Conquerors of the New Kingdom of Granada* (Albuquerque: University of New Mexico Press, 1995), 48–52.

evidence of nearby sources of gold and emeralds, were unlike anything they had seen elsewhere in the province of Santa Marta. But instead of returning to the coast to report their discovery to the man who had organized and funded the expedition, Santa Marta's governor, don Pedro Fernández de Lugo, Jiménez and his followers decided to delay their return. Perhaps they did not want to risk losing the spoils of their hard labor and suffering to the many newcomers who would flood the region upon hearing news of its riches. Over the next two years, and without contact or correspondence with any other Europeans, the entire expedition remained in Muisca territory. From roaming base camps, they circulated throughout the eastern highlands, driven by their quest to uncover the region's riches and collect booty. They even ventured far outside the Muisca realm to investigate rumors of gold-filled palaces and mysterious tribes of Amazon women. They formed alliances with some Muisca leaders, fought against others, and participated in joint military campaigns against the Muisca's fiercest enemies, the Panches. Remarkably, only six Spaniards died during the expedition's first thirteen months in Muisca territory, and none as a result of military conflict.

Of course, that the Spaniards did not lose a man in combat does not suggest that the "conquest" lacked violent encounters. Jiménez and his men regularly looted Muisca shrines or captured and tortured local leaders, from whom they demanded large ransoms. At times, such as when Jiménez and some of his followers seized the *cacique* (chief) of Tunja in August 1538, and with him a booty of more than 140,000 gold pesos and 280 emeralds, these strategies proved highly profitable. At other times, the Spaniards met fierce resistance; the region's most powerful ruler, often referred to simply as "the Bogotá," refused to submit to the authority of the newcomers or surrender any of his rumored treasure of gold and emeralds. His resistance cost him his life; and while Bogotá's successor, named Sagipa, established a brief alliance with Jiménez, his refusal, even under torture, to reveal the secret location of his predecessor's treasure ultimately cost Sagipa his life as well.

But even without Bogotá's fabulous riches, if indeed such a treasure ever existed, the conquistadors of New Granada all gained handsome rewards. By June 1538, when Jiménez decided it was time to divide the spoils and distribute the shares, the "official" booty exceeded two hundred thousand gold pesos and more than eighteen hundred emeralds. For the 173 foot soldiers and horsemen still alive when the shares were distributed, the expedition proved to be among the most profitable campaigns of the sixteenth century, perhaps second only to the conquest of Peru.

It was not until early 1539, almost three years after they had departed from Santa Marta, that Jiménez and his men had any contact with other Europeans. In fact, had it not been for the unexpected, and unwelcome, arrival of two other European expeditions, one from the governorship of Venezuela and the other from Quito, it is likely that Jiménez would have remained in the region even longer.[5] With the arrival of these competing factions, however, he decided it was time to return to Spain and submit his claims to the region before the Crown.[6] In a final act to bolster his position, Jiménez ordered the foundation of New Granada's first three towns, Santa Fe (de Bogotá), Tunja, and Vélez. After years of litigation, however, the Crown ultimately determined that the New Kingdom of Granada fell within the jurisdiction of the province of Santa Marta, and thus awarded the new discovery to Alonso Luis de Lugo, who, under the terms of a 1535 agreement (*capitulación*) with the Crown, had inherited the rights to the governorship from his deceased father, don Pedro Fernández de Lugo.[7]

Undoubtedly, the story of Gonzalo Jiménez de Quesada's expedition and the conquest of Muisca territory lacks the intrigue and dramatic flare of the Aztec or Inca conquest narratives.[8] In this tale, there were no scuttled ships, no pitched battles on magnificent island causeways, nor were captured Spanish conquistadors sacrificed atop great pyramids. And nothing in the tale of the conquest of Muisca territory matched the suspense of the Inca Atahualpa's

5. Nicolás Federmán led the expedition from the governorship of Venezuela, while Sebastián de Belalcázar's force arrived from the south. See Chapter 5 for more details.
6. While Jiménez never received the political power, wealth, or fame he felt he deserved, it was not long before it became clear that his expedition had found one of the richest and most densely populated regions of the Americas. Within a decade of his return to Spain, the Crown officially recognized the region's importance when it decreed in 1549 that a high court, or *audiencia,* should be established in Santa Fe. After a decade of legal problems stemming from his expedition, Jiménez returned to New Granada, where he resided until his death in 1579.
7. The full text of the agreement is translated in Chapter 2.
8. For Peru, John Hemming's *Conquest of the Incas* provides a readable narrative of the conquest. For Mexico, the most accessible popular account of the conquest of the Aztec Empire is Hugh Thomas, *Conquest: Montezuma, Cortés, and the Fall of Old Mexico* (New York: Simon and Schuster, 1993).

first encounter with Francisco Pizarro, with thousands of Inca warriors surrounding a Spanish force of fewer than two hundred. Quite simply, the Muisca have never captured public imagination on a level comparable to the Aztecs or the Incas. In fact, the same can be said for the Spanish protagonists in this tale. Few but the most serious scholars would recognize the names Antonio de Lebrija, Juan de San Martín, Antonio Díaz Cardoso, or Juan de Céspedes, all of whom figured prominently in this story. Even Jiménez de Quesada himself remains very much an enigmatic figure, one of many forgotten conquistadors hidden behind the long shadows of men like Hernando Cortés and Francisco Pizarro. Had the venerable nineteenth-century historian William Prescott, who wrote best-selling and highly entertaining accounts of the conquests of Mexico and Peru, agreed to write the history of the conquest of Colombia, perhaps the legacy of the Jiménez expedition would have been different.[9] Instead, it remains a story familiar to few.[10] Yet, despite the paucity of secondary accounts, the story of the conquest of the New Kingdom of Granada is still worth telling, if only to challenge some of the general assumptions about the nature of the Spanish Conquest of the New World and the conquistadors who participated in these early campaigns.

Through a series of sixteenth-century primary documents, translated into English for the first time, this book aims to reconstruct the compelling tale of the Gonzalo Jiménez de Quesada expedition and the early stages of the Spanish conquest of Muisca territory. What follows is a fragmented story, pieced together from multiple sources and told in numerous voices. In part, the decision not to privilege any single account of the expedition was unavoidable. The history of the conquest of Muisca territory never produced a Bernal Díaz del Castillo or a Pedro de Cieza de León, and no single account stands out

9. Colonel Joaquin Acosta (1800–52), a Colombian soldier and amateur historian and geographer, had approached Prescott to write a history of the conquest of New Granada. Acosta even offered all of his research materials, but Prescott declined, claiming he had already started working on his history of Philip II. See Sir Clements Markham, *The Conquest of New Granada* (Port Washington, N.Y.: Kennikat Press, 1912), 9.

10. Even recent surveys of Colombian history say little about the expedition. For example, see Frank Safford and Marco Palacios, *Colombia: Fragmented Land, Divided Society* (New York: Oxford University Press, 2002), 31–33; Anthony McFarlane, *Colombia Before Independence: Economy, Society, and Politics Under Bourbon Rule* (Cambridge: Cambridge University Press, 1993), 8–9; and David Bushnell, *The Making of Modern Colombia: A Nation in Spite of Itself* (Berkeley and Los Angeles: University of California Press, 1993), 8–10.

as the authoritative narrative of the conquest. And while there are some fine sixteenth- and seventeenth-century Spanish chronicles of the conquest,[11] they all were written many decades after the events had transpired; and more important, none of these colonial *cronistas* (chroniclers) were themselves participants in the Jiménez expedition.

The following story thus represents an effort to recover and reconstruct the details of one of the sixteenth century's greatest expeditions, told from the scattered testimonies and recollections of the Spanish participants themselves.

This project began as part of a broader examination of Muisca society in early colonial New Granada. In fact, I had never intended to write a history of the Gonzalo Jiménez de Quesada expedition; but after several months of research through thousands of pages of *probanzas de méritos*, or proof-of-merit petitions, I realized that this remarkable and long-neglected story needed to be told.

I am grateful to the University of North Florida for granting me a one-year sabbatical in order to complete this project. The research presented here was made possible through the generous financial support from the Program for Cultural Cooperation between Spain's Ministry of Culture and United States Universities, as well as a Franklin Research Grant from the American Philosophical Society. David Wilson deserves credit for his fine work on the maps that appear in this volume, and I also want to thank my student Kathleen M. Kole for her assistance in tracking down obscure sources and sending them to me while I was in Spain.

I owe special thanks to Matthew Restall for inviting me to contribute to this wonderful series, as both an author and as associate editor; I am also grateful for his insightful comments and suggestions. I would like to express my sincere gratitude to my friends and colleagues who helped to make research in Seville such a fruitful and enjoyable experience. Special thanks go to David Wheat, Mark Lentz, George Lovell, Leo Garofalo, and Rick Goulet. I would also like to

---

11. Among the best of these early chronicles are Castellanos's epic poem, *Elegías de varones ilustres de Indias* (1586) (Bogotá: Gerardo Rivas Moreno, 1997); Friar Pedro Aguado, *Recopilación historial*, 4 vols. (Bogotá: Empresa Nacional de Publicaciones, 1956–57); and Friar Pedro Simón, *Noticias historiales de las conquistas de tierra firme en las Indias Occidentales*, 7 vols. (1574–1627) (Bogotá: Banco Popular Español, 1981–82).

thank Renee Soulodre-La France, Jorge Gamboa, Kris Lane, Julián Ruíz Rivera, and Manuela Cristina García Bernal for commenting on an earlier version of this manuscript. I am particularly grateful for the friendship of Jeremy, Jane, Noah, and Ethan Baskes. Many thanks to the generous and helpful staff at the Archivo General de Indias in Seville. I could not have completed this project without the generous assistance of the finest paleographers I know, Esthér González Pérez, Guadalupe Fernández Morente, and Asmaa Bouhrass. It has been a pleasure working with Sandy Thatcher, Suzanne Wolk, and the entire staff at Penn State University Press; and I thank the anonymous reader, whose careful comments and suggestions were much appreciated.

My wife, Annie, gifted linguist, gourmet chef, and brilliant research assistant, deserves particular praise for her constant support and companionship. It is to her that I dedicate this book. Finally, I would like to thank my nephews, Charlie, John T., Rives, and Johnson, who never fail to challenge me to think of ever-more engaging tales of adventure.

[Cortés and Pizarro] did not discover or settle better or

richer provinces than I, even if the lands they conquered

were larger.

—Don Gonzalo Jiménez de Quesada, 1562

1

Introduction: The Other Andean Conquest

In 1528, eight years before Gonzalo Jiménez de Quesada's expedition
embarked on its journey up the Magdalena River, a Spanish vessel bound for Seville docked briefly in the port city of Santa Marta,
located on modern Colombia's Caribbean coast (see Map 1).[1] This
was not a rare occurrence; ships destined for Spain stopped in Santa
Marta with some frequency. But this particular vessel generated an
unusual amount of excitement among Santa Marta's residents. The
ship's exotic cargo included some unique treasures that had been
collected from somewhere along the Pacific coast of South America,
by a band of conquistadors led by Francisco Pizarro. Pizarro hoped
that these gifts would earn Crown favor and thus help him to secure
a royal contract (*capitulación*) to conquer the region for Spain. Of
course, these treasures, which included several strange New World
sheep,[2] only hinted at the fabulous riches that Pizarro and his followers would win when they returned to Peru four years later.

Rodrigo Alvarez Palomino, however, Santa Marta's governor at
the time, was so impressed by the 1528 cargo that he immediately
organized an expeditionary force to explore Colombia's interior in
an effort locate the source of these riches. Alvarez assembled three
hundred foot soldiers and fifty horsemen for the expedition, but
his untimely death doomed the venture before it even left Santa
Marta. Further attempts to launch overland expeditions from Santa

1. The epigraph is from servicios y méritos de Gonzalo Jiménez de Quesada, AGI
Patronato 155, N. 1, R. 14, fol. 740r. Jiménez often compared himself to Cortés and
Pizarro, and he considered the conquest of Muisca territory to be as important as the
conquests of Mexico or Peru. At the same time, his writings reveal a sense of bitterness
and despair over the fact that he never acquired the same level of fame or financial
rewards as the other two. In his 1576 *probanza*, written just three years before his
death, Jiménez boasted that he was considered the third-most important captain of the
conquest era, although he claimed that some ranked his conquest first in terms of quality and riches. See AGI Patronato 160, N. 2, R. 1, fol. 542r.

2. These so-called sheep (*ovejas*) were of course llamas. This story is told in the
anonymous "Relación de Santa Marta," AGI Patronato 27, R. 9, fol. 3v.

Marta failed to locate rich new lands, and all were plagued by severe shortages of men, money, and supplies. Thus, with the continued failures of expeditions into the interior, coupled with an increasingly hostile local indigenous population, Santa Marta faced possible abandonment.

Four years later, news of Pizarro's exploits in Peru reached Santa Marta's already disgruntled residents. This only served to make matters worse. With rumors of unimaginable riches to be had in the Inca realm, many of Santa Marta's inhabitants abandoned the province and made their way to Peru.[3] One of Santa Marta's residents later testified that the reports from Peru had sparked a mass exodus, leaving the coastal town virtually abandoned.[4] By early 1535, only nine horsemen and forty foot soldiers remained to defend the city from potential attacks from local natives, or from French or British pirates.[5] The city desperately needed a massive infusion of men and resources, without which the Crown risked losing what little presence it had along South America's northern coast.

The solution to Santa Marta's woes came from a most unlikely source. In late 1534 the sixty-year-old governor of the Canary Islands, *adelantado*[6] don Pedro Fernández de Lugo, sent his son Alonso to Spain to negotiate terms for the conquest and governorship of Santa Marta. Twice the Crown rejected Lugo's proposals, until at last the two parties reached an accord. In the final agreement, signed on January 22, 1535, don Pedro promised to recruit, organize, and equip an armada of seventeen hundred men to sail to Santa Marta. Furthermore, he committed to the construction of three fortresses to defend the town from attack, and he agreed to build six

3. See Juan Friede, "Antecedentes histórico-geográficos del descubrimiento de la meseta Chibcha por el licenciado Jiménez de Quesada," *Revista de Indias* 10, no. 40 (1950): 331–32.

4. Testimony of Juan Valenciano, servicios y méritos de Francisco Figueredo, AGI Patronato 155, N. 1, R. 8, fol. 439v.

5. Safford and Palacios, *Colombia*, 31.

6. In Castile, the office of *adelantado* dates back at least to the thirteenth century and the reign of Alfonso X; the holders of this title served as deputies to the Crown and held both civil and judicial powers over specific territories. Of the more than seventy individuals who successfully negotiated *capitulaciones* with the Crown in the sixteenth century, fewer than half were awarded the title of *adelantado*. See Clarence Henry Haring, *The Spanish Empire in America* (New York: Oxford University Press, 1947).

brigantines in order to launch an expedition to discover the source of the Magdalena River.[7] Eager to prevent the complete abandonment of the province, and at the same time promote further exploration of the South American interior, the Crown offered Lugo (and his son) a long list of concessions, including the governorship of all new lands conquered between Santa Marta and the South Sea (that is, the Pacific Ocean). Santa Marta's fortunes were about to change.

At the end of November 1535, after more than seven months of careful and costly preparations, don Pedro Fernández de Lugo's armada departed from the port of Santa Cruz on the island of Tenerife. In all, the armada consisted of no fewer than ten ships, which together carried somewhere between one thousand and twelve hundred passengers (among them a small number of women and black slaves).[8] After a brief stop on the island of Hispaniola to gather additional supplies,[9] the armada continued to Santa Marta, where it arrived to great fanfare and celebration on January 2, 1536. The new governor wasted no time in his effort to recoup the expenses he had incurred over the previous months. After several moderately profitable campaigns into nearby provinces, Lugo selected his lieutenant general, Gonzalo Jiménez de Quesada, to command an expedition up the Magdalena River.[10] In early April, just three months after his armada had arrived in Santa Marta, don Pedro sent the Jiménez expedition into the Colombian interior.

7. The complete terms of the first two proposals, as well as the final agreement between Lugo and the Crown, are translated below.

8. See Avellaneda Navas, *Conquerors of the New Kingdom of Granada*, 7–10. Lugo had agreed to take seventeen hundred men (fifteen hundred foot soldiers and two hundred horsemen) in his armada; in the end, he fell short in his efforts to recruit that number. In July 1535 the Crown issued a decree granting him a two-year extension on that commitment. Unfortunately, there is no known passenger manifest for the Lugo armada, and therefore we do not know exactly how many people, or even how many vessels, departed from Tenerife.

9. A letter from the Audiencia of Santo Domingo dated February 12, 1536, reported that Lugo's armada had arrived on the island more than a month earlier, and that it had purchased horses and other provisions before departing for Santa Marta. See AGI Santo Domingo 49, N. 44, R. 7, fol. 1v.

10. Unfortunately, little is known about the relationship between Pedro Fernández de Lugo and Gonzalo Jiménez de Quesada; it remains unclear how, when, and under what circumstances the two men met. Nevertheless, Lugo must have had a great deal of respect for and trust in Jiménez, whom he named his lieutenant general weeks before the armada sailed from the Canary Islands. See Avellaneda Navas, *Conquerors of the New Kingdom of Granada*, 9–10.

The New Kingdom of Granada

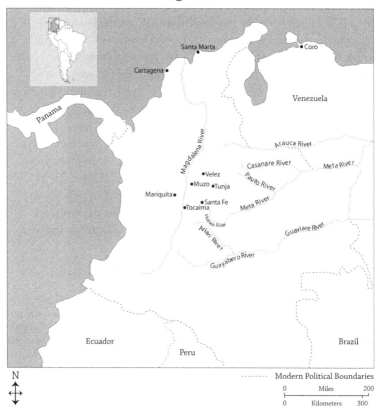

Santa Marta

Coro

Cartagena

Panama

Venezuela

Magdalena River

Arauca River

Casanare River

Meta River

Velez

Muzo

Tunja

Pauto River

Mariquita

Santa Fe

Meta River

Tocaima

Humea River

Guaviare River

Ar[a]ri River

Guayabero River

Ecuador

Peru

Brazil

N

Modern Political Boundaries

0	Miles	200
0	Kilometers	300

The Other Andean Conquest

It is unfortunate that the conquest of New Granada has not captured more popular or academic interest. Its influence on the broader historiography of the conquest era has been marginal at best. However, a closer examination of the Jiménez expedition reveals several important characteristics that challenge conventional wisdom about the conquest period in general and the lives of the conquistadors. For example, a brief comparison of the ages, previous New World experience, and attrition rates for Francisco Pizarro's forces (the "men of Cajamarca") and Jiménez's men forces us to reconsider some long-held notions about the conquest of the New World and the conquistadors who participated in it.

Previous New World military experience, or lack thereof, is one of several striking differences between Pizarro's men of Cajamarca and Jiménez's men of New Granada. For example, more than half of Peru's first conquistadors had at least five years of military experience in the New World. Furthermore, almost all the leaders of the expedition were hardened veterans; men such as Francisco Pizarro, Sebastián de Belalcázar, and Hernando de Soto had been in the Indies for two decades.[11] By contrast, with less than four months' experience in the Indies, Gonzalo Jiménez de Quesada was a true *chapetón*, an unseasoned and inexperienced newcomer to the Americas.[12] And he was not the only one. Of the ninety-three veterans of the expedition for whom we have data, only sixteen had more than five years of experience in the Indies. A handful had previous military experience in other parts of Europe,[13] but 63 percent of Jiménez's men had

11. James Lockhart, *The Men of Cajamarca: A Social and Biographical Study of the First Conquerors of Peru* (Austin: University of Texas Press, 1972), 23.

12. In his testimony of July 4, 1539, Gonzalo Jimémez de Quesada explained that most of the men on his expedition had died because they were *chapetones*. See AGI Patronato 27, R. 18, fol. 50v.

13. Before his arrival in the Indies at the age of twenty-one, Antonio Bermúdez had served for four years in Italy. Bermúdez was part of Juan Gaitán's company in Italy, Germany, Hungary, and Vienna. See servicios y méritos de Antonio Bermúdez, AGI Patronato 158, N. 1, R. 4, fol. 207v. Captain Gonzalo Suárez Rendón served in Italy and Hungary as well, under Pedro de Guzmán's company. See servicios y méritos de Gonzalo Suárez Rendón, AGI Patronato 156, R. 8, fol. 924r. Ortún Velasco, who served on one of the brigantines that sank at the mouth of Magdalena River, fought in Italy and Germany before making his way to Santa Marta in 1535. After his ship sank, Velasco chose to remain in Cartagena; however, he later joined Jerónimo Lebrón's

Table 1.1 Experience in the Indies

Years in Indies	Number of Men	
	Peru	New Granada
Almost none	37	59
Less than 5 years	12	18
c. 5	28	3
c. 10	14	12
c. 15	2	1
c. 20	7	
c. 25	1	
	101	93
Unknown	67	86
Total	168	179

practically no military experience at all. In fact, the vast majority, Jiménez among them, had only arrived in the Indies in January 1536, as part of Pedro Fernández de Lugo's ten-vessel armada. Thus, unlike either the Cortés expedition to Mexico or Pizarro's forces in Peru, the conquest of Colombia's eastern highlands was, for the most part, carried out by newcomers to the Americas.

Not only did Jiménez's men lack military experience in the Indies, but their inexperience was also combined with youth (see Table 1.2). Among Pizarro's men, roughly 31 percent (34 of the 107 men for whom there is evidence) were under the age of twenty-five when they arrived in Cajamarca in 1532; by contrast, of the 121 veterans of the Jiménez expedition for whom we have data, 55 percent fell into that category, with another 17 percent falling between the ages of fifteen and nineteen. The median age of the "men of New Granada" was only twenty-three.[14] This combination of youth and inexperience

1539 expedition to the New Kingdom. See servicios y méritos de Ortún Velasco, AGI Patronato 152, N. 3, R. 1. Captain Pedro Fernández de Valenzuela also was a veteran of the Italian wars. See Avellaneda Navas, *Expedición de Gonzalo Jiménez de Quesada*, 8.

14. In his detailed examination of the expedition and its participants, José Ignacio Avellaneda Navas concluded that the median age of Jiménez's men was twenty-seven, a figure also cited in Restall's *Seven Myths of the Spanish Conquest*, 37. It is worth noting, though, that Avelleneda based his calculation on the age at the time of arrival in the Muisca territory, and not at the time of departure from Santa Marta. Not only that, but his calculations came from a smaller body of evidence (104 samples as opposed to 121) than used here. See Avellaneda Navas, *Conquerors of the New Kingdom of Granada*, 62.

Table 1.2 Age at the Time of the Expedition

Age (Years)	Number of Men	
	Peru	New Granada
c. 15–19	5	20
c. 20–24	29	46
c. 25–29	41	28
c. 30–34	19	9
c. 35–39	8	16
c. 40–44	3	2
c. 45–49	1	0
c. 50–55	1	0
	107	121
Unknown	61	58
Total	168	179

perhaps explains why only 179 of the roughly eight hundred Spaniards on the expedition survived the twelve-month venture;[15] still, as we will see below, those who reached Muisca territory tended to live long lives. Not only that, but most veterans of the Jiménez expedition chose to remain in New Granada; only twenty men are known to have returned home to Spain, and no fewer than 108 decided to settle permanently in some part of New Granada.[16]

Perhaps the most striking difference between Pizarro's men of Cajamarca and the men of New Granada, and a topic that certainly merits further inquiry, is the dramatic variation in the attrition rates (see Table 1.3). Among Jiménez's men, the median age at death was more than sixty years old, astonishing for the sixteenth century and even more remarkable among conquistadors. No fewer than forty-two veterans of the expedition lived beyond the age of sixty-five, and half of those lived well into their seventies or early eighties. For reasons not yet fully understood, the conquistadors of New Granada enjoyed far longer lives than their counterparts in Peru and, most

15. Of course, the expedition was much larger than that; Jiménez and his men were also accompanied by an unknown number of native guides and carriers, a number of black slaves, and at least one Moorish slave. Unfortunately, there is no record of their numbers, ages, or fates.

16. See Juan Villamarín, "*Encomenderos* and Indians in the Formation of Colonial Society in the Sabana de Bogotá, 1537–1740" (Ph.D. diss., Brandeis University, 1972). In contrast to the situation in New Granada, roughly half of Pizarro's men decided to return to Spain. See Lockhart, *Men of Cajamarca*, 59.

Table 1.3 Rate of Attrition*

	Known no. of Men Still Alive	Date	No. of Years After Expedition
Peru	58	1536	4
	41	1540	8
	27	1545	13
	18	1550	18
	11	1560	28
New Granada	132	1540	4
	116	1544	8
	103	1549	13
	86	1554	18
	65	1564	28
	43	1574	38
	17	1584	48
	2	1594	58

* Using last known date alive

probably, elsewhere in the Americas. Of course, it is important to note that New Granada did not experience any of the bitter civil wars that claimed the lives of at least thirty-one of Pizarro's men before peace finally came to Peru in the 1550s.[17] Military conflicts, either between competing Spanish factions or against the Muisca population, were rare affairs in early colonial New Granada.[18] But it is unlikely that postconquest violence, or lack thereof, accounts for such a dramatic difference in the attrition rates of the two regions.

Perhaps more important than challenging some of the conventional wisdom about the conquistadors in general, a more rigorous examination of the conquest of New Granada forces us to reconsider several of the accepted notions of the Jiménez expedition itself. Even the purpose of the expedition should be subject to greater scrutiny. Most accounts of the conquest of New Granada explain that the expedition's aim was twofold: to discover an overland route to Peru, and to follow the Magdalena River to its source, which many believed would lead them to the South Sea. A 1537 letter from Santa Marta's town council to the Crown (translated in Chapter 2 of this volume),

17. See Lockhart, *Men of Cajamarca*, 61.

18. Minor uprisings did occur during the early years of Spanish rule, but these local revolts (in pueblos such as Ceniza, Suta, Tausa, Ocavita, Sogamoso, Garagoa, and Duitama) resulted in few Spanish casualties. See Sylvia Broadbent, "The Formation of Peasant Society in Central Colombia," *Ethnohistory* 28, no. 3 (1981): 262.

written just thirteen months after don Pedro Fernández de Lugo's death, certainly supports the claim that the Jiménez expedition had been sent to discover a path to Peru.

Indeed, news of Pizarro's exploits in Peru generated widespread excitement in the governorships of Cartagena, Santa Marta, and Venezuela.[19] In August 1533 the members of Santa Marta's *cabildo* (town council) sent a letter to the Crown explaining that local Spanish sailors were convinced that following the Magdalena River would lead to the South Sea and to Peru. Six months later, Santa Marta's governor, García de Lerma, reiterated this belief.[20] Similar letters were sent to Spain from the governorships in Cartagena, Venezuela, and even from the Audiencia (high court) of Santo Domingo.[21] For example, in a letter dated November 27, 1534, Santo Domingo's secretary, Diego Caballero, wrote a letter in which he urged the Crown to send at least five hundred Spaniards to Santa Marta. According to Caballero, not only would this lead to the opening of a land route from Santa Marta to Peru, it would also lead to the discovery of "many other Perus" that must exist between the two regions.[22] It is likely that Caballero's letter reached Madrid just as the Crown was finalizing the details of its agreement (*capitulación*) with don Pedro Fernández de Lugo.

While the discovery of an overland route to Peru would have appealed to the Crown, a careful examination of other documentary evidence reveals that the participants themselves probably had different motivations and expectations. In fact, it is unlikely that the men who volunteered to join the Jiménez expedition had much interest in plotting an overland route to Peru, a place that already had been conquered and settled by Spaniards; moreover, the spoils of the conquest had long since been divided among the fortunate few who had followed Pizarro from Panama. Likewise, the quest to find the Pacific

19. Two years before the Jiménez de Quesada expedition set out from Santa Marta, Cartagena's governor, Pedro de Heredia, sent an expedition, led by his son Antonio, to search for an overland route to Peru. Likewise, other expeditions were sent out to explore the interior of the governorship of Venezuela. But it was not until Jiménez's 1536 expedition that any venture from the northern coast of South America proved successful.

20. See Juan Friede, *Descubrimiento del Nuevo Reino de Granada y fundación de Bogotá* (Bogotá: Banco de la República, 1960), 45.

21. See "Carta del Audiencia de Santo Domingo, 20-10-1533," AGI Audiencia de Santo Domingo 49, R. 30, fol. 4r.

22. "Carta del secretario Diego Caballero a Su Magestad, 27-11-1534," ibid., 77, N. 81, fols. 1v–2r.

Ocean did not motivate men to invest their earnings and risk their lives on this venture. Instead, what Jiménez and his followers wanted was to find was a hitherto undiscovered "Peru," a "Cajamarca" of their very own. In fact, in the rich corpus of available documentary evidence, few veterans of the Jiménez expedition ever suggest that their mission was to discover an overland route to Peru, or to locate a river route to the South Sea. Instead, when asked about the purpose of the Jiménez expedition, most men simply stated that the goal was to discover *tierras nuevas*, new lands.[23]

Even Pedro Fernández de Lugo's motivation for authorizing the expedition was based on the desire to find new lands, and with them the profits needed to cover the debts he had incurred in mounting his armada. Of course, the search for an overland route from Santa Marta to Peru and the South Sea most certainly would have appealed to the Crown, something that Lugo used to his advantage in his negotiations to secure the rights to conquer the region, but that goal did not inspire Lugo himself. Jiménez and his men were sent out to win riches, and Lugo stood to earn 10 percent of all the spoils. Not only that, but one should not forget that Lugo had been granted the governorship of all new lands discovered between the city of Santa Marta and the South Sea. Most assuredly, then, Lugo was interested in reaching the South Sea, if only to determine the full extent of his governorship. Still, it is also worth noting that in Lugo's written instructions to Jiménez, drafted four days before the expedition departed from Santa Marta, there is no mention of Peru, nor are there any references to the search for the South Sea, let alone what the men should do if they succeeded in finding either.[24] Instead, of the fourteen instructions given to Jiménez, eleven addressed either the just treatment of the indigenous populations they should encounter or the nature in which all the gold (and other booty) should be acquired, recorded, and distributed.[25] Undoubtedly, the conquest of

23. There are dozens of testimonies from veterans of the Jiménez expedition who stated that the goal was to discover "new lands." For example, consider Juan de Olmos's testimony in servicios y méritos del capitán Antonio de Olalla, AGI Patronato 160, N. 2, R. 6, fol. 694v.

24. Lugo's final instructions to Jiménez have been transcribed by Juan Friede in *Gonzalo Jiménez de Quesada a través de documentos históricos* (Bogotá: ABC, 1960), 125–27, and in Friede, ed., *Documentos inéditos para la historia de Colombia [1509–1550]*, 10 vols. (Bogotá: Academia Colombiana de la Historia, 1955–60), 4:75–79.

25. Of the three remaining instructions, two outline what is to be done should the expedition encounter anyone from Venezuela or any of the Spaniards who had left

Peru provided powerful incentives to launch expeditions into undiscovered parts of the South American continent—but the participants who joined these ventures, and the governors who authorized and helped to fund them, did so in the hope of finding new riches of their own.

As the opening paragraph of the preface suggests, narrative accounts of the Jiménez expedition bear a striking resemblance to the Peruvian conquest narrative—the timing, the Andean backdrop, the numbers of men involved (168 in Peru, 179 in New Granada), as well as the captured *cacique*, his promised ransom, and his subsequent execution. These are all shared features of both conquest narratives. A closer examination of the conquest of New Granada reveals far more differences than similarities, however. Perhaps the most enduring misconception of the Spanish conquest of Muisca territory involves the story of the indigenous civil war, and its influence on the eventual outcome. Interpretations of the conquest of Peru and the conquest of New Granada both emphasize the importance of the bitter civil unrest at the moment Spaniards first arrived. And while there is indisputable evidence of such a conflict between Atahualpa and Huascar in the Inca realm, there is no compelling evidence in either Spanish or Colombian archives to support the occurrence of a civil war in Muisca territory. Future scholarship may prove otherwise, but the so-called Muisca civil war between the Zipa of Bogotá and the Zaque of Tunja appears to be nothing more than an invention of later Spanish chroniclers (none of whom participated in the conquest), whose treatment of the conquest of New Granada simply borrowed from the Peruvian conquest narratives. Curiously, despite the lack of corroborative evidence, historians have never questioned the veracity of the Zipa-Zaque civil war, and it continues to be repeated in virtually every treatment of the Spanish conquest of New Granada.

Readers will note that none of the primary documents that follow, which represent some of the earliest firsthand accounts of the conquest story, makes any reference to a civil war between the *caciques* of Bogotá and Tunja. Not only that, but readers will also notice (in Chapter 5) that when Bogotá's ruler, Sagipa, offered his allegiance

---

Santa Marta eight months earlier. The other instruction orders that in the event of Jiménez's death, Captain Juan de Junco should lead the expedition; and if he should die, Captain Gonzalo Suárez Rendón would become captain general.

Muisca Territory

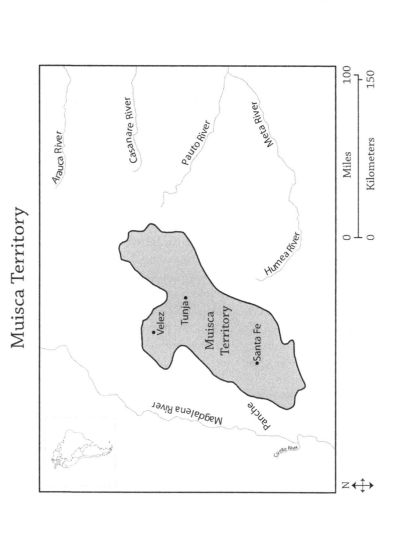

to Jiménez in exchange for Spanish military assistance, it was not to launch a campaign against Tunja but rather to fight against Bogotá's real enemies, the Panches. Until more convincing evidence emerges, the common perception that the conquest of Muisca territory was facilitated by an internal civil war between the Zipa and the Zaque should thus be viewed with deep suspicion.

The Sources

As mentioned earlier, no single account stands out as the authoritative voice on the conquest of New Granada, but the absence of such a voice should not suggest that there is a paucity of documentary evidence on the subject. What follows, then, is a reconstruction of the Jiménez expedition and the conquest of Muisca territory, told from the perspectives of seven different sixteenth-century primary documents.[26] Five of the documents included in this study appear in their entirety; two others have been abridged slightly. Readers will note that most of the book is based on three lengthy accounts, namely, the anonymous "Relación de Santa Marta" (probably written by Captain Antonio Díaz Cardoso circa 1545), Captain Juan de San Martín and Captain Antonio de Lebrija's "Relación del Nuevo Reino" (1539), and the "Epítome de la conquista del Nuevo Reino de Granada." Excerpts from all three of these accounts appear in Chapters 2, 3, and 4 in order to maintain a clear chronology of the events as they unfolded and to facilitate a comparative examination of the sources. Detailed footnotes also have been added throughout the translations, many from the vast body of colonial *probanzas de méritos*, or "proof-of-merit" petitions.[27] Brief introductions to each chapter establish the

26. All but one of the documents included in this study were located in the Archivo General de Indias (AGI) in Seville, Spain. The one exception, the "Epítome de la conquista del Nuevo Reino de Granada," is located in the Archivo Histórico Nacional de España in Madrid. However, facsimile copies of the entire Epítome can be found in Carmen Millán de Benavides, *Epítome de la conquista del Nuevo Reino de Granada: La cosmografía española del siglo XVI y el conocimiento por cuestionario* (Bogotá: CEJA, 2001), 123–29; and in Demetrios Ramos Pérez, *Ximénez de Quesada en su relación con los cronistas y el epítome de la conquista del Nuevo Reino de Granada* (Seville: Escuela de Estudios Hispano-Americanos, 1972).

27. New Granada's conquistadors left scores of documents, including thousands of pages of colonial *probanzas;* these neglected sources offer rich details about the expedition and the early years of Spanish occupation of Colombia's eastern highlands.

historical context for the documents that follow, and in some cases an additional preface has been added for further clarification.

The story begins in late 1534, with don Pedro Fernández de Lugo's negotiations with the Crown for the rights to the conquest and governorship of the province of Santa Marta. The three documents in Chapter 2 include don Pedro's initial petition, his son Alonso's amended proposal, followed by the final agreement (*capitulación*), signed in late January 1535. Chapter 3 picks up the story fourteen months later, shortly after the Lugo armada has arrived in Santa Marta. The four documents in Chapter 3 include short excerpts from the two Relaciones, the Epítome, and a 1537 letter from the town council (*cabildo*) of Santa Marta. All four documents chronicle the first stage of the Gonzalo Jiménez de Quesada expedition, a seven-month period that begins with the departure of Jiménez's ground forces on April 5, 1536, and ends as Jiménez and two hundred followers abandon their route up the Magdalena River and begin their climb into the eastern highlands.

Chapters 4 and 5 include excerpts from the same three sources, namely, the two Relaciones and the "Epítome de la conquista del Nuevo Reino de Granada." Chapter 4 follows the few surviving members of the expedition across the Opón Mountains and into Muisca territory, where they arrive in early March 1537. It also contains a lengthy section from the Epítome, which provides rich details of Muisca culture and society. The fifth and final chapter, the longest in the book, chronicles a two-year period bound roughly by the Spanish sacking of the Muisca pueblo of Tunja in August 1537 and Jiménez de Quesada's return to Spain in early July 1539. This period witnessed some of the most dramatic and tragic events of the conquest, such as Bogotá's murder, the military campaigns against the Panches, the distribution of the booty, and the search for the Amazon women. Two of the three documents translated in Chapter 5 also chronicle the circumstances surrounding the capture, arrest,

---

Piecing the conquest story together from colonial *probanzas* is a challenging and laborious task, however, in part because *probanza* testimonies for New Granada rarely sustained a coherent narrative flow. For more details about the characteristics and conventions of colonial *probanzas* and their potential value to historians, consider Murdo J. MacLeod, "Self-Promotion: The Relaciones de Méritos y Servicios and Their Historical and Political Interpretation," *Colonial Latin American Historical Review 7*, no. 1 (1998): 25–42; and Restall, *Seven Myths of the Spanish Conquest*, 12–14.

The Routes of the Expeditions

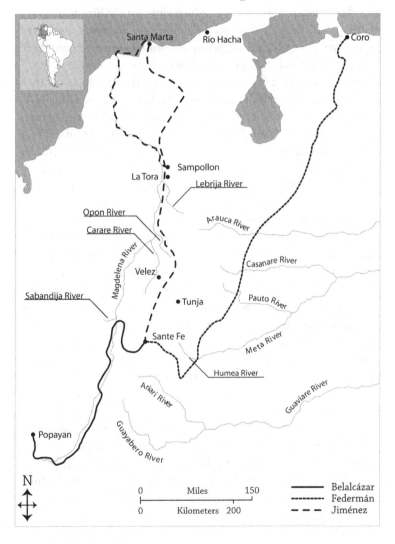

Santa Marta • Rio Hacha • Coro •

Sampollon
La Tora •
Lebrija River

Opon River

Carare River

Arauca River

Magdelena River

Velez •

Casanare River

Sabandija River

• Tunja

Pauto River

Sante Fe •

Meta River

Humea River

Ariari River

Guaviare River

Popayan •

Guayabero River

N

| 0 | Miles | 150 |
| 0 | Kilometers | 200 |

——— Belalcázar
••••••••• Federmán
– – – Jiménez

torture, and subsequent death of Bogotá's successor, Sagipa. And all three sources end with the arrival in New Granada of the two other expeditionary forces, one from Venezuela, led by Nicolás Federmán (Nikolaus Federmann), the other from Peru, under the command of the conquistador Sebastián de Belalcázar. For Jiménez, the unexpected arrival of competing groups of conquistadors led all three men to return quickly to Spain to press their claims to this newly discovered region, and it is with their departure for Spain that the accounts end.

One final note of caution before proceeding—as valuable as the following sources are for helping to piece together the details of the Jiménez expedition and the subsequent exploration, conquest, and colonization of Muisca territory, it is important to acknowledge their significant silences. Spanish accounts reveal virtually nothing of the scores of black slaves, or native carriers, guides, cooks, and translators, all of whom played important if forgotten roles in this story. And although some of the accounts that follow, the Epítome in particular, include some of the earliest descriptions of Muisca culture, including details of their religious beliefs and practices, diet, weapons, clothing, and government, these descriptions are all presented from Spanish perspectives. Not only that, but the accounts reveal almost nothing about the multitude of non-Muisca peoples who resided along the Magdalena River; the only other native group discussed in any detail are the Panches. Spanish descriptions of Panche society are highly untrustworthy, however, and should be read with great care. As a people who resisted both Muisca and Spanish incursions into their territory, the Panches have been treated very unkindly by colonial documents. In the few accounts where they are discussed, the Panches are judged harshly, often reduced by Spanish observers to nothing more than naked cannibals whose daily lives were motivated by their quest for human flesh. It is most unfortunate that for New Granada there exist none of the native accounts of the conquest period that have so enriched the historiography of other parts of the Americas.[28] Sadly, then, in the story that follows, the voices of Muiscas and Panches remain silent.

---

28. For two recent examples, see James Lockhart, *We People Here: Nahuatl Accounts of the Conquest of Mexico* (Berkeley and Los Angeles: University of California Press, 2000); and Matthew Restall, Lisa Sousa, and Kevin Terraciano, eds., *Mesoamerican Voices: Native Writings from Colonial Mexico, Oaxaca, Yucatan, and Guatemala* (Cambridge: Cambridge University Press, 2005).

It is because of wealth that we have witnessed and will continue to see many victories, great conquests and discoveries of great empires that have been hidden from us. This is seen each day, under commanders who, with royal powers, have thus occupied themselves, with desire to show themselves serving their king and embarking on campaigns of great risk, labor, and expense, spending their personal wealth with no one else's help; for, as has been said, it is he alone who gathers the people, the arms, the pay, and the sustenance, and because of this, it is most important to be wealthy.

2

Three *Capitulaciones*: Don Pedro Fernández de Lugo
and the Governorship of Santa Marta

It is important to recognize that the Spanish Crown never possessed
the resources to fund the exploration, conquest, or settlement of the
New World.[1] Instead, Spain's monarchs often negotiated private agreements with individuals or corporations, offering financial rewards,
offices, and titles to those who organized, equipped, and funded these
early ventures. Over the course of the sixteenth century, the Crown
entered into more than seventy of these private agreements, known in
Spanish as *capitulaciones*. Such contracts helped push the boundaries of
Spain's American possessions and at the same time mitigate the threats
of Portuguese, French, and English expansion in the New World.

This chapter contains three documents related to Pedro Fernández de Lugo's negotiations with the Crown over the governorship of
the province of Santa Marta. It opens with Lugo's initial proposal,
dated September 2, 1534, in which he promised to recruit, arm, and
transport 1,150 men (150 of them horsemen) for the (re)conquest
and (re)settlement of Santa Marta. In addition, Lugo vowed to build,
at his own expense, three fortresses to protect the city. He also committed himself to the construction of six brigantines, which he agreed
to send to explore the Magdalena River. In return for these services,
Lugo requested a long list of concessions, including the governorship of Santa Marta, and with it a handsome annual salary. However,
don Pedro's son Alonso, who had been sent to Spain to present the
terms before the Crown, must have learned that his father's terms
were unacceptable. Ten days before royal officials in Madrid officially
reviewed the details of the initial proposal, don Alonso submitted a
series of alterations. Thus, the second document below, dated November 16, 1534, outlines the list of amendments; not only did don
Alonso increase the number of men don Pedro would have to commit
to the venture, he also lowered the concessions requested from the

1. The epigraph is from Captain Bernardo de Vargas Machuca, *The Indian Militia
and Description of the Indies* (1599), ed. Kris Lane, trans. Tim Johnson, manuscript,
2006.

Crown. A complete translation of don Alonso's revised proposal is then followed by the final *capitulación*, signed January 22, 1535.

While the agreements reveal a great deal about the expectations and motivations of don Pedro, his son, and the Crown, the *capitulaciones* can be somewhat misleading and must therefore be read with caution. In spite of his position as governor of the Canary Islands, don Pedro was not in a position to fund the entire armada on his own. In order to finance this ambitious venture, he needed partners. Thus, while Alonso de Lugo traveled to Seville to recruit men, gather equipment, and negotiate the armada's costly transportation across the Atlantic, don Pedro worked to secure additional financing. In May 1535 don Pedro reached an agreement with two Italian merchants, both residents of Tenerife, to split the costs of the armada.[2] Juan Alberto Gerardini and Cristóbal Francesquini agreed to divide equally the expenses of Lugo's venture, in return for an equal share of Santa Marta's future profits over the next three years.[3]

Unfortunately for don Pedro, most of the spoils of the conquest of Santa Marta found their way into other pockets. In fact, Lugo never learned the fate of the expedition he had worked so hard to organize and fund.[4] On October 15, 1536, just six months after the Jiménez expedition had departed, Santa Marta's elderly governor was dead.

A Proposal Made

AGI Patronato 27, R. 15, bl. 6, fols. 3r–6r (September 2, 1534)

In the name of God almighty and of his mother, our Lady the Virgin Mary, and of the archangel Michael, and lord Santiago, patron of

2. The same two Italian merchants, Juan Alberto Gerardini and Cristóbal Francesquini, had also helped to finance Diego de Ordas's expedition to Marañón and Paria. Ordas (and many others at the time) believed that gold would be found closer to the equator, a belief that may help to explain why Lugo sought to secure a *capitulación* for the conquest of Santa Marta. See Leopoldo de la Rosa Olivera, "Don Pedro.Fernández de Lugo prepara la expedición a Santa Marta," *Anuario de Estudios Atlánticos* 5 (1959): 414–16.

3. See Avellaneda Navas, *Conquerors of New Granada*, 7. The only exception to this agreement concerned the extraction of pearls; don Pedro paid half the cost of the extraction and thus was entitled to 50 percent of all profits. Gerardini and Francesquini each received 25 percent.

4. Lugo died on October 15, 1536, almost five months before the Jiménez expedition reached Muisca territory. It was not until March 1539 that Jiménez himself learned of the governor's death.

Spain. What follows is a petition from don Pedro Fernández de Lugo, *adelantado* of the Canary Islands, in which he explains what he can do on Your Majesty's behalf in the conquest of Santa Marta and the discovery of the Río Grande, and what he requests from Your Majesty in return for his services:

First, for the said conquest [the *adelantado*] says that he will take one thousand foot soldiers from the [Canary] Islands and Castile, among them crossbowmen, harquebusiers, musketeers, and shield bearers, and that he will supply all the necessary armaments.

Furthermore, he says that he will take another one hundred and fifty horsemen, and saddled mares, all equipped with the necessary armaments.

He states that he will transport these foot soldiers, horses, and mares all the way to Santa Marta, and supply them with food and drink until they arrive.

He also claims that he will construct, at his own expense, three fortresses in the location or locations that he believes would best serve Your Majesty's interests; he states that this will be done within the first five years of his arrival.

He says he will construct six brigantines, all equipped with sails, oars, and everything else necessary to carry out the discovery of the Río Grande; and he states that this will be done within a timeframe that he considers propitious.

In return for the services listed above, *adelantado* Lugo requests that Your Majesty grant him the following:

First, that Your Majesty grant him the governorship of the province of Santa Marta, [the borders of] which extend from Cartagena to [Venezuela], and all the way down to the South Sea; Lugo asks that this be granted to him and to his descendants in perpetuity, and that he be named Captain General, with the powers of Viceroy, over all the conquered territory.

As governor and captain general, he asks that Your Majesty grant him an annual salary of six thousand *castellanos*;[5] naturally, Your Majesty will include a provision that the salary be paid from the royal revenues generated from the lands conquered, without any other payment from Your Majesty. And that the officials in charge of the royal treasury keep record of the payments.

5. A *castellano* was a gold coin worth approximately 485 *maravedíes*, the smallest and most common measure of Castilian currency. See Hugh Thomas, *Rivers of Gold: The Rise of the Spanish Empire from Columbus to Magellan* (New York: Random House, 2003), 552.

That Your Majesty pay him each year, and in perpetuity, six percent, or up to two million [*castellanos*], of all royal revenues generated from the conquest, be they from *almojarifazgos* (customs duties), the royal fifth, or any other means of regular or supplementary revenue belonging to Your Majesty and to all the monarchs who succeed him; and that this be recorded in the royal books, with all the clauses and signatures that the *adelantado* requests so that he can pass these privileges to his descendants or anyone else with legal claim.

That Your Majesty grant him and his descendants in perpetuity [the office] of *alguacilazgo mayor*.[6]

That Your Majesty grant an annual salary of five hundred *castellanos* to pay the salary for a lieutenant, because there will be much work and many risks, and such a person will be deserving of it.[7]

That Your Majesty permit that during the *adelantado*'s lifetime he be permitted to name and train *regidores*,[8] judges and public notaries and all other offices named later; he asks that Your Majesty grant him this authority.

That Your Majesty authorize that for the duration of his life, Lugo can issue *repartimientos*[9] and grant residence to the conquistadors and settlers of the said land, and that he be permitted to give grants of Indians, lands, water, and other properties as he sees fit; he assures that he will be mindful to grant each individual what he deserves. And he requests that these grants be just as legally binding, in perpetuity, as if Your Majesty had awarded them himself.

6. Chief constable.

7. The final *capitulación* between Pedro Fernández de Lugo and the Crown makes no reference to this particular request; nevertheless, it is worth mentioning that on November 10, 1535, while still in the Canary Islands, Lugo appointed Gonzalo Jiménez de Quesada to serve as his lieutenant in the province of Santa Marta. Unfortunately, we know nothing about the relationship between Jiménez and Lugo at that time. How, when, and where the two men met is unknown. See Juan Friede, *Invasión del país de los Chibchas: Conquista del Nuevo Reino de Granada y fundación de Bogotá* (Bogotá: Tercer Mundo, 1966), 121; and Rosa Olivera, "Don Pedro Fernández de Lugo," 422–23.

8. A *regidor* was a junior council member who served in the municipal council, or *cabildo*. See Matthew Restall, "Cabildo," in *Iberia and the Americas: Culture, Politics and History*, ed. J. Michael Francis, 3 vols. (Santa Barbara, Calif.: ABC-Clio, 2006), 1:165.

9. The term *repartimiento*, which literally means "distribution" or "division," was used in several different contexts in colonial Spanish America. In this context, as the rest of the passage reveals, *Adelantado* Lugo is requesting the authority to distribute land grants to deserving Spaniards and to allocate Indians in *encomienda* grants.

For each one of the fortresses that he constructs or that already exist, he requests that Your Majesty provide, in perpetuity, an annual salary of 200,000 *maravedíes*[10] for the maintenance and defense of each fortress; and that Your Majesty supply each fortress with artillery and munitions, as well as artillerymen, a salary to pay them, as well as a supply of some half culverins, with the remaining artillery consisting of falconets [*falcones*] and wrought-iron breechloaders [*versos*].

From everything that is conquered, won, and pacified, that Your Majesty grant the *adelantado* and his descendants forty leagues square of land, not necessarily the best land available, but not the poorest either; [in this land, Lugo] and his descendents will enjoy civil and criminal jurisdiction in the same manner as the great lords of Castile. And although Your Majesty holds royal sovereignty over this land, as he does over the lands of the great lords of Castile, he will not have the right to collect tributes of any kind, including the *alcabala*,[11] and the *almojarifazgo*. May it please Your Majesty to grant him the title that best serves Your Majesty's interest.

That Your Majesty concede that no more than the *diezmo* [one-tenth tax] be paid on all gold mined during the first ten years; each year thereafter the tax will increase [by one-tenth], from one-ninth to one-eighth and so forth until it reaches the royal fifth [*quinto*]. The royal fifth will be paid on all goods acquired through warfare or trade.

That Your Majesty concede that the conquistadors, settlers, and residents of the newly conquered lands be exempt from having to pay the *alcabala* or any other taxes or tribute.

That Your Majesty concede that the conquistadors and settlers be exempt from the *almojarifazgo* on all domestic goods that they bring for their homes [from Spain].

After the first fortress has been built, which will be done at [the *adelantado's*] expense, he asks that Your Majesty pay him one-fifth of the construction costs in the first year, another fifth in the second year and so on and so forth until five years have passed and the

10. At the time, the Spanish used several different currency denominations. The *marevedí* (a copper coin) was the smallest and most commonly used currency in sixteenth-century Castile. But there were others. For example, one *real* was equivalent to thirty-four *maravedíes*. A gold *ducado* was worth 375 *maravedíes*, while one silver *peso* was worth 450 *maravedíes*, and, as mentioned earlier, one *castellano* was valued at 485 *maravedíes*. See Thomas, *Rivers of Gold*, 551–53.

11. The *alcabala* was a sales tax collected by the Crown. See Kendall Brown, "Alcabala," in Francis, *Iberia and the Americas*, 1:57–58.

entire cost of the fortress has been paid. Payments for the other two fortresses will follow the same manner. And if all three fortresses are built within the first year or two, then Your Majesty will pay the costs [in a single installment?] from his royal treasury.

He asks that Your Majesty postpone the appointment of any prelate to serve in the lands discovered and colonized, until the territory has been settled and pacified; and he requests that Your Majesty issue this decree in writing. This is necessary in order to prevent the clergy from burdening the conquistadors with such demands until they are granted specific license from Your Majesty to receive *diezmos*.

That Your Majesty decree that no individual be permitted to trade in the territory without direct license, and that over the first ten years, Your Majesty collect no more than the *diezmo*.

That Your Majesty order that don Alonso Luis de Lugo and his father be paid back-salaries owed to them from the year 1520 to the present, which will appear in the official account books; this is what I want and what I deserve in order to assist with the enormous expenses I am incurring for this conquest.

That Your Majesty grant him what little booty remains in Seville from the supply that initially was destined for Maluco;[12] most of [that plunder] has been spent already, and Your Majesty allocated some of it for the expedition to Río de la Plata.[13]

That Your Majesty grant him power and authority over rebellious Indians who refuse to become Christians and loyal subjects of Your Majesty; and that having duly been informed [of the consequences of their actions],[14] war can be waged, by fire and by sword, and that those captured can be bound and sold.

That Your Majesty concede that [in civil matters] litigants may appeal to the *cabildo* in cases that do not exceed three hundred

---

12. In the Philippine Islands.

13. No specific names are mentioned in this document, but the reference to Rio de la Plata surely concerns Pedro de Mendoza's 1536 expedition to the region. Two years earlier, in 1534, King Charles I granted Mendoza authority to equip and lead a force to conquer the eastern coast of South America. In September 1535 the Mendoza armada stopped briefly in the port of Santa Cruz (Canary Islands), before departing for Rio de la Plata. Unfortunately, Lugo makes no specific reference to the nature or value of the plunder awarded to Mendoza; it is unlikely that Lugo was granted this request because the final *capitulación* makes no further mention of it.

14. Here *Adelantado* Lugo is making reference to the *requerimiento*, or Require-ment. Drafted in 1513 by the Spanish jurist Juan López de Palacios Rubios, the *requerimiento* outlined Spain's divine and legal claim to the new lands and asked

castellanos; and that he [Lugo] be given jurisdiction over all criminal cases, except those that involve murder or dismemberment.

That Your Majesty grant authority to the royal officials who serve as public notaries in Your Majesty's service, that they may appoint replacements in their offices.

That Your Majesty award don Pedro Fernández de Lugo the governorship of the islands of Tenerife and La Palma, with the title of *adelantado*, which, upon his death, will be inherited by his son don Alonso.

Should Your Majesty decide it in his best interest to order my return [to Spain] and not proceed with the armada, Your Majesty shall reimburse all of my expenses, as well as the expenses of those who accompany [me on this conquest]. Because of the fact that this is a new conquest, may it please Your Majesty to grant the *adelantado* immunity in civil and criminal judicial proceedings, and their corresponding legal punishments, for all such cases that Your Majesty deems appropriate. The *adelantado* assures that he will take great care to do what is in the best interest of God and of Your Majesty.

If it should be our lord God's will to take don Pedro Fernández de Lugo from this present life before he is able to carry out the conquest, or while he is engaged in it, Your Majesty should transfer this agreement to don Alonso, his son.

That Your Majesty grant don Pedro Fernández de Lugo the title of *adelantado* of the province of Santa Marta, from sea to sea, to him and to his descendents.

That Your Majesty concede that whatever benefits are granted by your judges and royal officials are hereditary in nature because [your officials] will take great care to assure that the recipients are capable and well deserving.

In order to guarantee the integrity and authenticity of this entire agreement, [the *adelantado* requests] that a document be drafted on which Your Majesty signs his royal name and stamps his royal stamp, with all the necessary entails and signatures. [This document] shall be retained by the *adelantado* and his heirs.

Signed: Fernández de Lugo

---

native leaders to submit to the authority of the Spanish Crown and the pope. If they refused, just war could be waged against them; this standard plea for submission was supposed to be read to all natives before any military engagement. See Restall, *Seven Myths of the Spanish Conquest*, 19, 87.

If another governor or conquistador from neighboring regions, or from anywhere else for that matter, were to enter the said territory, either to conquer or for any other reason, that Your Majesty issue by royal decrees that they not be permitted to enter; should they do so, that they be ordered to leave at once, and that I be allowed to administer their sentences, capture them, and send them back to Your Majesty.

Read in Madrid November 26, 1534.

A Proposal Revised

AGI Patronato 27, R. 15, bl. 4, fols. 8r–9v (November 16, 1534)

I, don Alonso Luis de Lugo, on behalf of my father don Pedro Fernández de Lugo, *adelantado* of the Canary Islands, state that in [my father's] name I presented an agreement of everything that he offered to do on his part, and what grants he requested from Your Majesty in return. And so that you see how much desire he possesses to serve Your Majesty in this expedition, which is the conquest of Santa Marta, I have amended the terms of the agreement. In his name, I offer the following:

First, my father the *adelantado* will take 1,500 foot soldiers from Castile and the Canary Islands, [among them] riflemen, crossbowmen, arcabusiers, and shield bearers. In accordance with the difficult challenges [they will face] in that land, they will all be well armed and equipped with all the necessary munitions.

He will take two hundred horsemen, all well armed and fully equipped.

He says that he will transport all these people at his own cost, providing them with food and drink and paying the costs of the fleets until they arrive in Santa Marta. He will also sustain them for the first four months, without Your Majesty having to spend anything until then.

Within five years of his arrival in the province, the *adelantado* will construct, at his own expense, three fortresses, in the parts of the province where they will prove most advantageous.

For the discovery of the Río Grande, he will build, at his own expense, six brigantines, equipped with sails and oars and everything else necessary at the time.

In return for the above-mentioned services, the *adelantado*, and I in his name, beg Your Majesty the favor of the following:

That Your Majesty grant him the governorship of the province of Santa Marta, which extends from the province of Cartagena to the province of the Germans [Venezuela] down to the South Sea, with the title of Captain General and Viceroy for him and for his descendents in perpetuity, or at least for two lives.

That Your Majesty compensate the *adelantado* with an annual salary of three thousand *castellanos*, to be paid from the province's royal revenues.

That Your Majesty pay him each year and to his descendents in perpetuity four percent, or up to two million [*castellanos*], of all royal revenues in the province.

That Your Majesty grant him and his descendants in perpetuity the office of *alguacilazgo mayor* in the province.

That during his life, the *adelantado* be authorized to appoint *regidores*, notaries, *jurados*, and other offices from among the conquistadors whom he considers suitable.

That you grant him authority that he may issue land and water grants to the conquistadors. These land grants can be up to four *caballerías* and four *solares* each,[15] depending on the quality of the recipient; and they are to be theirs in perpetuity.

That Your Majesty grant him 100,000 *maravedíes* for the maintenance and occupation of each fortress that he builds.

For all that is conquered and pacified, that Your Majesty grant him twenty leagues square of land, not necessarily the best land available nor the worst; and that the soil, land, mountains, and water, over which he and his descendents will have civil and criminal jurisdiction, reserving for Your Majesty the taxes, royal incomes and rights.

That in the first ten years, only the *diezmo* be paid on all gold taken from the mines; each year thereafter the tax will increase until it reaches one-fifth. The royal fifth tax will be paid on everything else acquired through warfare or barter.

That over this same ten-year period, the conquistadors and settlers be exempt from having to pay the *alcabala* or any other taxes or

---

15. Here Lugo is requesting permission to reward individuals up to four land grants, with each parcel (*solar*) measuring up to four *caballerías*, roughly the equivalent of 382 acres.

tribute, as well as the *almojarifazgo* on personal domestic goods and provisions that they bring [from Spain].

That no individual be permitted trade goods in the territory of this conquest without your license [from the Crown]; thus, Your Majesty's interests and royal incomes will be served and protected.

That [Your Majesty] grant him the authority to wage war, by fire and sword, against all Indians who, having been duly notified [of the consequences], rebel [against Your Majesty's service]; and that he [have the authority] to take them as captives.

That all the royal officials, such as public notaries, who take part in the conquest, can name replacements for their offices.

Seeing that I too will serve in the same conquest, that on my father's death Your Majesty grant me, don Alonso, the title of *adelantado* of the Canary Islands, with the governorship of Tenerife and La Palma, as my father has [at present].

Should Your Majesty decide it in his best interest to order [my father's] return [to Spain] before the conquest or after having arrived there, Your Majesty shall reimburse all expenses as well as the expenses of those who accompany [him].

That Your Majesty grant my father the title of *adelantado* of the said province, from sea to sea, for him and for all of his descendents.

That Your Majesty order that it be determined the salary my father is owed for the governorship he possesses, and that the money be drawn from the royal incomes of the said province because my father wants it in order to serve Your Majesty.

That for the conquest Your Majesty grant him license to remove from these kingdoms and from Andalucía up to one hundred horses and mares, and that he be permitted to take any kind of livestock without penalty.

That Your Majesty grant the province and settlers [of Santa Marta] the same privileges that have been extended to other lands and islands, as best serves you.

If another governor or conquistador from neighboring lands, or from anywhere else, were to enter the province to conquer, or are within its borders, that Your Majesty order that they leave; and that my father, the *adelantado*, have the authority to arrest them and send them to Your Majesty.

If it should be our lord God's will to take my father, the *adelantado*, from this present life before he is able to carry out the conquest, that this agreement and contract be protected, and transferred to me, don Alonso, his son.

Don Alonso Luis de Lugo[16]

An Agreement Reached

"Capitulación del gobierno de Santa Marta con Pedro Fernández de Lugo" (January 22, 1535), AGI Patronato 27, R. 12, fols. 1v–4r

First, I hereby grant license and authority to don Pedro Fernández de Lugo, *adelantado* of the Canary Islands, on our behalf and in our name and in the name of the Royal Crown of Castile, to conquer, pacify and colonize the lands and provinces still left to be conquered, pacified and colonized in the province of Santa Marta. The province of Santa Marta extends [westward] to the borders of the province of Cartagena, whose conquest and governorship we have entrusted to Pedro de Heredia,[17] [and eastward] to the borders of the province of Venezuela, whose conquest and governorship has been entrusted to the Germans Bartolomé and Antonio Welser.[18] From there, [the province of Santa Marta] extends south all the way to the South Sea,

16. Less than one month later, on December 14, 1534, don Alonso submitted another petition to the Crown in which he reiterated some of the earlier demands from his November proposal and added several others. In addition to his previous requests that he and his father be given authority to issue land grants of up to four *caballerías*, that he and his father be awarded back pay, and that no other governor or conquistador be permitted to enter into their jurisdiction, Lugo made four additional pleas. He asked that they be given license to take up to four hundred slaves to Santa Marta; he requested permission to take all the ships he deemed necessary from the Canary Islands; he asked that no other captain be permitted to recruit people or take horses from the Canary Islands until after the Lugo armada had departed for Santa Marta (this request was firmly denied); and he requested that he be awarded the habit of the Order of Santiago. See AGI Patronato 27, R. 15, bl. 5, fol. 11r.

17. In the late 1520s Pedro de Heredia served as Governor Pedro de Vadillo's lieutenant in the province of Santa Marta. On his return to Spain in 1530, Heredia petitioned the Crown to grant him authority to carry out the conquest of the province of Cartagena. Two years later, on August 5, 1532, Heredia signed his *capitulación* with the Crown; the newly appointed governor of Cartagena departed from Spain at the end of September 1532. See María del Carmen Gómez Pérez, *Pedro de Heredia y Cartagena de Indias* (Seville: Escuela de Estudios Hispano-Americanos, 1984), 10–11.

18. In 1528 King Charles I granted the governorship of Venezuela to the commercial house of Welser, giving them authority to explore, settle, and exploit the resources

provided that you do not enter the boundaries or jurisdictions of any other province that has been granted to any other governor. In recognition of his obedient service on our behalf, and in order to pay him due honor, we promise to make the said *adelantado* our governor and captain general of Santa Marta and the towns within its borders for all the days of his life, with an annual salary of one million *maravedíes*, which he is to enjoy from the day he and his people set sail from one of the ports in the Canary Islands to carry out the conquest. The salary is to be paid from our royal revenues and taxes generated in the province. During his tenure as governor and captain general he is to colonize and conquer the territory; if this should not occur, we are not obligated to pay him anything whatsoever.

We want and we order that when it is our lord God's pleasure to take the *adelantado* don Pedro Fernández de Lugo from this present life, that you, Alonso Luis de Lugo, should inherit the governorship and captaincy general of the province for all the days of your life, with the annual salary of one million *maravedíes* in accordance with [the same terms], and in the same manner, in which your father, the *adelantado*, holds it.

Furthermore, we grant the *adelantado* don Pedro Fernández de Lugo the title of our *adelantado* of the lands and provinces that are discovered and populated. Upon your father's death, you, don Alonso Luis de Lugo, are to inherit this title.

Furthermore, I give him license to construct, in accordance and agreement with our officials in the province, two fortresses within the borders of the territories discovered and colonized. They are to be built in locations that he and our royal officials consider necessary for the defense and pacification of the lands and provinces. And we grant him an annual salary of 75,000 *maravedíes* for the maintenance and occupancy of each fortress. [These fortresses] are to be built at his own expense; we are not obliged to pay for them, nor are any of the monarchs who follow us. Once our royal officials deem them fully operational, the salary for each fortress is to be paid from the fruits of the land.

Furthermore, you, don Alonso Luis de Lugo, on behalf of your father don Pedro Fernández de Lugo, have requested that we grant

---

found in the province. For more information on this German commercial house, which had offices in the 1520s in both Seville and in Santo Domingo, see Avellaneda Navas, *Conquerors of the New Kingdom of Granada*, 14–19.

you a certain number of [Indian] vassals from the new lands and provinces that you happen to discover and pacify. As far as this request is concerned, we have decided to wait until we receive detailed reports about the new lands that you discover and colonize. In the meantime, in order to compensate you for your hardships and your services, we decree that you are to receive an annual share of one-twelfth of all benefits that pertain to the Crown, excluding [revenues from lands] already discovered and pacified. However, before you receive your share, you are to pay all the expenses and salaries incurred by our royal officials in the conquest.[19]

Furthermore, in order to assist you with the costs of transporting the people for the conquest,[20] we will reward you with a payment of four thousand gold *ducados*,[21] to be paid by our officials from the taxes and benefits that we receive from the lands and provinces conquered.

We give you permission to issue land grants to the residents and settlers of the lands and provinces that are conquered and colonized, in the same manner as our governors in other provinces of our Indies have done before, and continue to do.

We give license so that [Lugo], or anyone else to whom he gives authority, can transport one hundred black slaves from our kingdom, or from the Kingdom of Portugal and Cape Verde Islands, to Santa Marta.[22] At least one-third must be females;[23] and you shall be exempt from all applicable taxes that belong to us [in such

19. On November 5, 1535, less than one month before the Lugo armada departed from the Canary Islands for Santa Marta, Pedro Fernández de Lugo decided to reward his son, Alonso Luis de Lugo, for having successfully negotiated the terms of the *capitulación* and for having recruited the men for the expedition. The *adelantado* agreed to give his son one-fifth of the one-twelfth share that he had been awarded by the Crown. This agreement between father and son was to last four years, beginning with the launch of the first expedition from Santa Marta. See Rosa Olivera, "Don Pedro Fernández de Lugo," 417.

20. Several members of the Lugo armada later testified that they had to pay between twenty-five and thirty *ducados* each to cover the costs of food and transportation. For example, see servicios y méritos de Diego Rincón, AGI Patronato 165, N. 1, R. 3, fol. 136r.

21. A gold *ducado* was worth 375 *maravedíes*.

22. In a petition dated December 12, 1534, Alonso Luis de Lugo asked permission from the Crown to take as many as four hundred slaves to Santa Marta. See AGI Patronato 27, R. 15, bl. 5, fol. 11r.

23. In this particular version of this agreement, or *capitulación*, found in AGI Patronato 27, R. 12, fol. 3v, the notary erroneously writes the word *hombres* (men), instead of *hembras* (females). Another copy of the very same agreement, located in AGI Santa Fe 1174, L. 2, fol. 35v, corrects this error.

circumstances]. Should you sell them all, or even some of them, on the islands of Hispaniola, San Juan, or Cuba, or anywhere else for that matter, you will forfeit these exemptions, which then must be paid to our royal treasury.

We will send orders to grant [adelantado Lugo] permission, as is customary, to take as many as three ships currently docked in the Canary Islands. [These ships, and their captains] must have some familiarity and knowledge of the Indies; and/or they must be willing to sail there.[24] These vessels must be free of commitments to any other armada. And the owners of these vessels are to be paid a just fee.

One of the conditions is that, as far as the pacification, conquest, settlement, and treatment of the Indians is concerned, your father, the adelantado, is required to follow and obey to the letter, all that is proclaimed in the laws and instructions that we have issued, and anything else that [we] decree.

This agreement is made with your father, the said adelantado, on the condition that when he departs from the Canary Islands on this conquest and colonization, he takes with him any and all religious [clergy] that we assign to the task of instructing the native Indians of those lands in Our Holy Catholic Faith.[25]

He is not to carry out the conquest without them. And he is to pay the costs of their passage, their provisions, and all other necessary maintenance costs, in accordance with their character. He is to incur all of these expenses over the course of the entire voyage, without taking from them anything whatsoever. We entrust that he will do this and comply with our orders, as it serves both God and us; should he do differently, we will consider it a great disservice.

In accordance with the rights and laws of our kingdoms, when our subjects and the captains of our armies happen to capture some prince or lord from the lands where, under our orders, they are at war, the ransom collected from that lord or cacique,[26] as well as all

24. Again, there is some discrepancy between the two primary accounts of this agreement. In one version the notary writes *y* (and), while in the other he writes *o* (or).

25. It is unclear how many clergymen, if any, were part of the Lugo armada, but it appears that only two members of the clergy, Antón de Lezcamez and Friar Domingo de Las Casas, joined Gonzalo Jiménez de Quesada's 1536 expedition from Santa Marta. See servicios y méritos de Antón Lezcamez, AGI Patronato 158, N. 1, R. 1, fols. 4v, 10r.

26. Adopted from the Arawakan word for ruler, *kussiquan*, the term *cacique* was used throughout most of Spanish America to refer to local dynastic rulers. See Richard Conway, "Caciques," in Francis, *Iberia and the Americas*, 1:167–68.

of his private possessions, belong to us. However, in consideration of the great hardships and difficulties that our subjects endure in the conquests of the Indies, and in order to reward them for their services and offer them some compensation, we declare and order that should you happen to take some *cacique* or lord captive, then his treasures of gold, silver, precious stones, and pearls that you acquire, either through ransom or in any other manner, that you give us a share of one-sixth. The remainder should be divided among the conquistadors, having first paid the royal fifth. In the event that the said *cacique* or principal lord should die in battle, or later through the legal process, that we be given half of his belongings. This payment shall be issued before any of the costs incurred by our royal officials are reimbursed. The other half shall be divided [among the conquistadors], once again after the royal fifth is paid.

In the Villa de Madrid, January 1, 1535.

They endured a great many hardships, and starvation, until
[at last] they reached the town they call Cuatro Brazos [La
Tora]. [Along the way,] the Indians engaged them in warfare.
Some [Spaniards] were killed by caimans or by tigers; others
died from the injuries they suffered from having to walk
about barefoot and naked. Out of sheer hunger, they would
eat lizards, snakes, mice and bats.

3

By Land and by Sea: From Santa Marta to La Tora

In early January 1536, almost one year after he had secured the governorship of Santa Marta, don Pedro Fernández de Lugo's armada, numbering roughly one thousand people, arrived in Santa Marta.[1] Eager to recover the costs he had expended over the past twelve months, Lugo wasted no time in dispatching expeditions into the surrounding regions. But these ventures yielded few financial rewards, and with conditions in Santa Marta rapidly worsening, Lugo decided to turn his attention to the exploration and discovery of the Magdalena River. To that end, he determined to mount a two-pronged expedition; the first consisted of a ground force of roughly five hundred men (including horsemen) who were ordered to follow the river's course overland. To provide logistical support, Lugo sent another two hundred men, who sailed west from Santa Marta in five brigantines and then entered the mouth of the Magdalena River. The two forces departed separately but agreed to meet at a settlement called Sompallón, located one hundred leagues from the coast, and then continue upriver together. To lead this ambitious expedition, Lugo turned to his second in command, Gonzalo Jiménez de Quesada.

1. The epigraph is from servicios y méritos de Diego Gutierrez Pimental, AGI Patronato 161, N. 1, R. 1, fols. 1r–1v. It is worth noting that Gutierrez was not part of the Jiménez expedition, but his maternal grandfather, Diego Romero, was, and Gutierrez hoped that by emphasizing his grandfather's services, the Crown would reward him with the inheritance of Romero's *encomienda*. Furthermore, in preparing his petition, it is clear that Gutierrez had read his grandfather's own *probanza de mérito* from 1561, in which Diego Romero testified that many Spaniards on the Jiménez expedition "died from wounds they received from Indians, or were killed by caimans and tigers; some perished from the wounds they suffered from walking barefoot and naked. Others died from eating lizards, snakes, mice and bats." See servicios y méritos de Diego Romero, AGI Patronato 154, N. 3, R. 1, fol. 503v. On the arrival of Lugo's armada in Santa Maria, see Avellaneda Navas, *Expedición de Gonzalo Jiménez de Quesada*, 3. A letter from the Audiencia of Santo Domingo, dated February 12, 1536, confirms that the Lugo armada arrived in Santa Marta in early January. The same letter indicates that several of Lugo's ships previously docked in Santo Domingo, where they purchased some horses and picked up supplies. See Carta de la Audiencia de Santo Domingo, AGI Santo Domingo 49, R. 7, N. 44, 1v.

Jiménez's ground force, which was divided into eight companies, departed from Santa Marta on April 5, 1536. Less than two weeks later, on Easter Saturday, the five brigantines began their journey west toward the Magdalena River. A terrible storm arrived, however, just as they reached the mouth of the river. At least two of the vessels sank; the others were badly damaged. Many of the survivors made their way to Cartagena and refused to return to Santa Marta. But the disaster did not deter don Pedro de Lugo; Santa Marta's governor acted quickly to refit another five vessels. The second attempt to enter the Magdalena River proved successful, and by July 1536 the brigantines had reached Sampollón, where they reunited with Jiménez's ground forces.

With the arrival of the brigantines, the expedition received much-needed reinforcements and provisions. Jiménez transferred the injured and the infirm to the brigantines, and the joint forces continued the journey upriver. The advance was slow, however, hindered by heavy rains, strong currents, and flooding, coupled with the thick mud and jungle vegetation along the banks of the Magdalena River. When they finally reached the native settlement of La Tora in October 1536, Jiménez decided to wait until the rains subsided.

For three months the expedition remained in La Tora, plotting its next step and searching for alternative routes into the interior. With supplies dwindling and the mortality rate rising, Jiménez dispatched several reconnaissance missions to search for provisions, and perhaps for signs of rich new lands. Explorations upriver revealed nothing but more flooding and difficult terrain—but several small expeditions to the east found promising signs; they returned to La Tora with reports of good trails on which local natives carried blocks of salt and rich cotton *mantas* (blankets). The source of these goods appeared to come from somewhere up in the eastern highlands.

Finally, after nearly eight months following the Magdalena River, Jiménez and his captains decided to change course. With a force of two hundred men, Jiménez began the long climb up the western flank of Colombia's eastern highlands. The injured and infirm were left with the brigantines, having agreed to wait six months for Jiménez's return. But the men who remained with the brigantines reneged on the accord and within weeks were back in Santa Marta; more than two years would pass before they learned the fate of those who had joined Jiménez.

The four selections presented in this chapter chronicle the first stage of the Jiménez expedition, a nine-month period from early April to December 1536. Unfortunately, little is known about this first stage of the Jiménez expedition, and the documents below offer few details. The expedition's official logbook, which recorded (in theory) all the booty collected during the expedition, reveals that the search for riches yielded little. Over an eight-month period the logbook recorded only eight entries, with a total booty of just 9.5 pesos and 2 *tomines* of *oro fino*, and 72.5 pesos and 9.5 *tomines* of *oro bajo*. While the profits were low, the same cannot be said of Spanish casualties. One hundred men lost their lives in the four months it took to travel between Santa Marta and Sompallón; and another one hundred died before the expedition finally reached La Tora.[2] More Spaniards died during the three-month stay in La Tora. Still others, perhaps as many as fifty men, were ordered to remain behind with the brigantines and await Jiménez's return.[3] Thus, by late December 1536, when Jiménez began to cross the Opón Mountains and into Muisca territory (chronicled in Chapter 4), his force had dwindled from eight hundred to just two hundred Spaniards.

Excerpt from the "Epítome de la conquista del Nuevo Reino de Granada," fols. 2–3

The "Epítome de la conquista del Nuevo Reino de Granada" is a curious text. Discovered in 1889 by the Spanish historian Marcos Jiménez de la Espada,[4] the Epítome has attracted a great deal of attention from Colombian historians, most of whom have attributed it to Gonzalo Jiménez de Quesada.[5] However, in her recent analysis of the account, Carmen Millán de Benavides convincingly argues that Gonzalo Jiménez de Quesada was not the author. According to Millán, the Epítome represents a multitude of accounts and testimonies collected by Charles V's royal historian and cosmographer Alonso de

2. See Avellaneda Navas, *Expedición de Gonzalo Jiménez de Quesada*, 24.

3. As we will see in the next chapter, the men who remained behind did not wait long. Following an attack by local natives, the brigantines sailed back to Santa Marta.

4. The only surviving copy of the Epítome is located in Madrid at the Archivo Histórico Nacional de España, Sección Documentos de Indias, 27. See Millán de Benavides, *Epítome de la conquista del Nuevo Reino*, 3.

5. In 1972 historian Demetrios Ramos Pérez published a detailed study of the Epítome in which he concluded that Jiménez was its author.

Santa Cruz (1505–67).[6] For Millán, the Epítome's choppy and confusing nature, which has led some scholars to conclude that the surviving copy is an incomplete version of a lost manuscript, is instead the careful notes and summaries Santa Cruz had compiled in order to create a historical atlas of the world. And while Jiménez's own responses probably were included in the text, his voice is but one of many layered into the text. Santa Cruz probably gathered information not only from the participants in the Jiménez expedition but also from some of the men who arrived in Muisca territory in 1539 with Sebastián de Belalcazar and Nicolás Federmán.

Nothing in the text gives clear evidence as to when it was written, but it was probably finished at some point between 1547 and 1550. The Epítome's final page (translated in Chapter 5) makes references to recent titles and offices conferred on Gonzalo Jiménez de Quesada in 1547, namely, the title of *mariscal* and a magistrate's post in Santa Fe. It never refers to Jiménez as *adelantado*, a title he received in 1565. Furthermore, Santa Cruz himself wrote that he had stopped writing about New Granada before 1551.

Readers should note that the section below is only the opening excerpt; the rest of the text appears in Chapters 4 and 5 of this volume.

Between the provinces of Santa Marta and Cartagena flows a river that divides the two provinces; they call it the Magdalena River. However, it is more commonly referred to as the Río Grande, because in truth, this river is very grand indeed. The fury and violence with which it crashes into the sea is so great that it pushes fresh water one league into the sea.[7] The various governors and captains of the

---

6. An important clue to the identity of the Epítome's author is scribbled near the top of the opening page, a page that most scholars simply have overlooked because at first glance it appears to be of little significance. Written in various hands, the first page includes a list of cities in New Granada and little else. However, it also includes the phrase "Del arca de Santa Cruz" (from Santa Cruz's chest). After Santa Cruz's death in 1567, the Epítome passed to his successor, Juan López de Velasco (c. 1530–98), who may have used it as a model for the famous questionnaires (the *relaciones geográficas*) sent to solicit information about the history and geography of Spain's colonial possessions in the Americas.

7. It was not until 1532, just four years before the Jiménez expedition, that the Portuguese navigator Jerónimo Melo became the first European to enter the Magdalena River directly from the sea. Melo led a small expedition, with two caravels and fifty men, and sailed roughly thirty-five leagues up the Magdalena River before turning back to the coast. See Friede, "Antecedentes histórico-geográficos," 337; and Avellaneda Navas, *Expedición de Gonzalo Jiménez de Quesada*, 5.

two provinces of Santa Marta and Cartagena always have ventured upriver in search of new lands and provinces. Of course, more people from Santa Marta have carried out these expeditions because Santa Marta, beginning with Bastidas's governorship,[8] was colonized long before Cartagena.[9] However, no Spaniard from either province had ever journeyed upriver more than fifty or seventy leagues. The farthest anyone had made it was to the province they call Sompallón, which is an Indian settlement located on the bank of the said river. On the few occasions that the Spaniards reached Sompallón, they did not venture ahead, in spite of the fact that their Indian guides and translators always spoke of the great riches, large provinces, and the lords who ruled them, that would be found much farther upriver. However, in spite of these rumors, on the occasions that the Spaniards made it as far as Sompallón, they stopped there.[10] At times they refused to continue upriver because already they were satisfied with

8. A native of Seville, Rodrigo de Bastidas first explored the coast of Santa Marta in 1500, when he and the other Spaniards with him bartered with local natives for gold and pearls. More than twenty-five years passed before Bastidas returned to Santa Marta, this time as governor. During the first decades of the sixteenth century, Santa Marta attracted few Spaniards; those who did venture along Colombia's Caribbean coast did so in search of slaves, gold, and, on occasion, pearls. Despite the fact that the region fell loosely under Governor Pedrarias Dávila's jurisdiction in Panama, there was no permanent Spanish presence in Santa Marta until the mid-1520s. In November 1524 the Crown reached an agreement (*capitulación*) with Rodrigo de Bastidas, entrusting the new governor with the conquest and settlement of the province and port of Santa Marta. Bastidas was to take at least fifty Spaniards to settle the new town, fifteen of whom were supposed to take their wives with them. Bastidas's tenure as governor did not last long; upset that the governor refused to distribute all the gold they had acquired, Bastidas's lieutenant, Pedro de Villafuerte, and several of his supporters, stormed the governor's house late one night and attacked him. Bastidas survived the attack, but his wounds were severe. The injured governor was taken to Santo Domingo to seek medical attention, but he never reached Hispaniola; Bastidas died from his wounds in Cuba in January 1527. See Friede, *Descubrimiento del Nuevo Reino*, 11. Also, see Gómez Pérez, *Pedro de Heredia*, 2–4; and Avellaneda Navas, *Conquerors of the New Kingdom of Granada*, 3. For details of the 1524 agreement between Bastidas and the Crown, see Friede, *Documentos inéditos para la historia de Colombia*, 1:76–81. Bastidas's tenure as governor and his death are also discussed in the anonymous "Relación de Santa Marta," AGI Patronato 27, R. 9, fols. 1v–3v.

9. In 1533, roughly seven years after the foundation of Santa Marta, Pedro de Heredia founded the city of Cartagena.

10. It is worth noting that Juan de San Martín and Juan de Céspedes, both of whom later served as captains on the Jiménez expedition, were also captains on a 1534 expedition that reached Sompallón. At that point the expedition, which consisted of 150 foot soldiers and horsemen, and 140 men in one caravel and three brigs, turned toward

riches they had won or had peddled with the Indians; on other occasions, they simply were unable to advance because torrential rainfall had muddied all the land along the river bank, thus blocking the route they needed to follow upriver. The truth of the matter is that the Spaniards could have overcome these obstacles if it were not for the fact that the people from Santa Marta already were quite content with their discoveries in La Ramada, a small but rich province located close to Santa Marta itself.[11] And this satisfaction with La Ramada continued until eventually the Spaniards took everything from it and left it in ruins, showing no consideration for public or private welfare, but rather, motivated only by their own interests. Likewise, Cartagena's residents were perfectly satisfied with the ample quantities of gold they took from the tombs they uncovered in Cenú, located close to Cartagena.[12] But they too exhausted all the riches, as those from Santa Marta had done in La Ramada. Thus, the people from the two provinces were left with nothing more than the hope of what might be discovered upriver, rooted in the many rumors and stories they had heard from their Indian translators. However, the people from Santa Marta and Cartagena were not the only ones to hear such tales; similar accounts had reached both the governorship of Venezuela, which had been colonized by the Germans, as well as the people in Urapari.[13] They all had heard great rumors from their Indian translators of a powerful and rich province called Metha, which, based on

the Cauca and San Jorge rivers before returning to Santa Marta. For more details of these early expeditions up the Magdalena River, see Avellaneda Navas, *Expedición de Gonzalo Jiménez de Quesada,* 5–7.

11. Spanish expeditions to La Ramada began as early as Rodrigo de Bastidas's arrival as governor in 1526, and they continued with some frequency over the next decade. Located along the coast, roughly thirty leagues from Santa Marta, La Ramada boasted large numbers of deer, as well as a rich supply of gold. One expedition, during Garcia de Lerma's tenure as Santa Marta's governor, returned from La Ramada with treasure worth more than forty thousand pesos, as well as a great number of slaves. See "Relación de Santa Marta," AGI Patronato 27, R. 9, fols. 2v–11v. Various sixteenth-century descriptions of La Ramada can be found in Hermes Tovar Pinzón, *Relaciones y visitas a los Andes: S. XVI,* vol. 2, *Región del Caribe* (Bogotá: Colcultura, 1993).

12. For more detailed information on the early Spanish exploration and exploitation of Cenú, see Gómez Pérez, *Pedro de Heredia.* It is also worth noting that Pedro de Cieza de León, the "prince of Peruvian chroniclers," arrived in Cartagena in 1535 and was a veteran of some of the first campaigns into Cenú. See Pedro de Cieza de León, *The Discovery and Conquest of Peru,* ed. and trans. Alexandra Parma Cook and Noble David Cook (Durham: Duke University Press, 1998), 6–7.

13. Urabá?

the directions the Indians gave them, must have been located somewhere near the headwaters of the Río Grande. However, the people
from Venezuela were unable to follow the river's course inland, as
those from Santa Marta and Cartagena could do; instead, they had
to cross overland within the limits of their own territorial jurisdiction. And as it turned out, these myriad reports, which had generated
such excitement and eagerness among residents from one end of the
northern coast to the other, all referred to the same place, namely, the
New Kingdom of Granada, which was discovered and colonized by
the *licenciado* Gonzalo Jiménez de Quesada, who was destined to do
so. And everything unfolded in the following manner. In the month
of April of the year 1536, Gonzalo Jiménez de Quesada, who at present is *mariscal*[14] of this New Kingdom, departed from the coastal
city of Santa Marta to explore the Río Grande. He took with him six
hundred soldiers, divided into eight infantry companies, as well as
one hundred horsemen. Furthermore, certain brigs were dispatched
to pursue Jiménez and his men upriver, and offer assistance to those
traveling overland along the river's edge.[15] The infantry captains
whom Jiménez brought with him were named Captain Juan de San
Martín, Captain Juan de Céspedes, Captain Pedro Fernández de
Valenzuela, Captain Lázaro Fonte, Captain Antonio de Lebrija, Captain Juan del Junco, and Captain Gonzalo Suárez; the other company
fell under the command of the *licenciado* Captain General Jiménez.[16]
The captains of the brigs that sailed upriver were Captain Gómez

14. Gonzalo Jiménez de Quesada was granted the title of *mariscal* on May 21,
1547. See AGI Contratación 5787, N. 1, L. 2, fol. 139v.

15. The strategy of sending certain brigs to support (and sell merchandise to)
overland expeditions was not unique to Gonzalo Jiménez de Quesada's expedition.
Previous governors, including Pedro de Badillo, had done the same. See "Relación de
Santa Marta," AGI Patronato 27, R. 9, fol. 4r.

16. With an average age of thirty, the eight captains who led the overland expedition represented a blend of expertise and inexperience. It is not surprising that Juan de
San Martín, Juan de Céspedes, and Antonio de Lebrija played such central roles over
the course of the twelve-month expedition; between them they had roughly thirty-five
years of experience in the Indies, and all three had led or participated in earlier explorations of the Colombian interior. Their collective expertise proved crucial to Jiménez.
Another captain, Juan de Junco, had almost two years of experience in Colombia; Junco
had also been in Río de la Plata. The four remaining captains, Pedro Fernández de
Valenzuela, Lázaro Fonte, Gonzalo Suárez Rendón, and Jiménez de Quesada, had virtually no experience in the Indies, but both Suárez Rendón and Fernández de Valenzuela
had served in Spain's military campaigns in Italy. It should also be noted that the

de Corral, Captain Antonio Díaz Cardoso, and finally Captain Juan de Albarrazín.[17] This entire armada was organized under the volition, and with the consent, of don Pedro de Lugo, who at that time was governor of Santa Marta. Don Pedro de Lugo, *adelantado* of the Canary Islands and father to the current *adelantado,* don Alonso Luis de Lugo, had been appointed governor of Santa Marta following the death of the previous governor, Garcia de Lerma.[18] The *adelantado* don Pedro de Lugo named Jiménez as Captain General and second in command. However, don Pedro died days after *licenciado* Jiménez departed on the said conquest, thus leaving *licenciado* Jiménez in charge of all matters related to that province of Santa Marta.[19]

Having departed on the conquest, *licenciado* Jiménez spent more than one year exploring upriver, following along the banks of the Río Grande; he ventured more than one hundred leagues farther than any other Spaniard before him. Eventually he ended up in a place

---

account fails to mention another captain, Juan de Madrid, who died during the course of the expedition. For further information on the backgrounds of these captains, see Avellaneda Navas, *Expedición de Jiménez de Quesada,* 8–9.

17.   There were in fact five brigantines, not three, that sailed up the Magdalena River to join the overland force. Here the Epítome neglects to mention that the river forces were led by another *licenciado,* Diego Hernández Gallegos, a native of Gibraltar. The account also fails to mention Captain Juan de Chamorro. Perhaps the reason for the omissions is that neither captain was present when Jiménez and his men finally reached Muisca territory. Both captains remained behind in La Tora (with the injured and infirm) when the Jiménez expedition moved up the eastern highlands. At some point during their return to Santa Marta, Captain Chamorro was killed in an Indian attack. In terms of their backgrounds, the captains of the brigs were slightly older than the other captains. At thirty-six, Antonio Díaz Cardoso was the only one under forty at the time of the expedition (Gómez de Corral and Gallegos were both forty-two, and Juan de Albarrazín was forty; Chamorro's age remains unknown). And as far as experience in the Indies goes, Captain Chamorro (with two years) and Captain Cardoso (with eight) appear to have been the only two with previous experience in the New World. Finally, we do not know the precise number of men who sailed in these five brigantines, but José Ignacio Avellaneda Navas suggests that the vessels could have carried a total of 250 people. See ibid., 9.

18.   García de Lerma served as Santa Marta's governor from 1528 (although he did not arrive from Spain until 1529) until his death in 1534. Following Lerma's death, Doctor Rodrigo Infante was sent from Santo Domingo to serve as provisional governor until Pedro Fernández de Lugo arrived, but Doctor Infante died just months after his arrival in Santa Marta.

19.   Gonzalo Jiménez de Quesada did not learn of Lugo's death until 1538, when Sebastián de Benalcazar and his men arrived from Peru and informed Jiménez of the governor's death.

called La Tora,[20] also known as Pueblo de los Brazos, located roughly one hundred and fifty leagues from the point where the mouth of the Magdalena river meets the sea. It had taken a long time to reach La Tora, a result of the great difficulties encountered along the way, the path often blocked by terrible flooding or the thick vegetation along the coast of that river. The *licenciado* and his men decided to spend the winter in La Tora because the river was raging with such fury that they could go no further; moreover, the waters were so high that they could not walk along its banks. Therefore, Jiménez sent some brigantines upriver to explore because, as just mentioned, it was impossible to walk along the riverbank. The brigantines sailed twenty leagues ahead, but they returned with nothing but bad news; they found that the river had burst so far beyond its banks that there were none but a few Indian settlements, and some small islands. The only other thing they could see was water. Seeing that there was little point in continuing upriver, the *licenciado* decided to explore a small tributary nearby, which flowed into the Río Grande. It appeared that this tributary flowed down from the hills and high mountains located on the left side of the Río Grande. We later learned, following our exploration, that they called these mountains the sierras de Opón.[21]

During the entire journey up the Río Grande, before we ever reached La Tora, we carried with us a certain expectation, which was this: that the salt that is consumed by all the Indians up and down the river came from the sea, along the coast of Santa Marta, and that this salt is exchanged upriver, moving from one group of Indians to another. This salt is granular, and through trade networks it reaches as far as seventy leagues from the coast. However, by the time the salt reaches that far, it is in such small supply that it becomes extremely

20. The origin of this term is unclear. Some scholars, including Juan Friede, have suggested that Gonzalo Jiménez de Quesada gave the town its name, fueling speculation that Jiménez's ancestors were Jews or *conversos*. At present, however, we know too little about his background in Spain to confirm or deny this suspicion. See Friede, *Gonzalo Jiménez de Quesada*, 18. And while most participants later referred to the place as La Tora, Los Brazos, or Los Cuatro Brazos, one veteran of the expedition, Juan Ramírez de la Hinojosa, claimed that the men named the town Barrancasbermejas [*sic*], its modern name. See servicios y méritos de Juan Ramírez de la Hinojosa, AGI Patronato 158, N. 3, R. 1, fol. 311r. Another participant in the expedition, Juan de Montalvo, also testified that the Spaniards called the town either Los Cuatro Brazos or Barrancas Bermejas. Ibid., fol. 377v.

21. The Sierra del Opón is located in the modern Colombian department of Santander.

expensive among the Indians; and thus, no one but the most principal chiefs consumes it. All the other Indians make their own salt by blending human urine with palm [nut?] powder. Beyond the seventy leagues, we came across another kind of salt, which is not granular like the other; instead, it is packed into large blocks, like sugar loafs. And the farther we climbed upriver, the less value the Indians attached to those salt blocks. For that reason, and seeing the differences between one type of salt and the other, it became perfectly clear that the grain salt came up from the coast, whereas the other salt came downriver. And owing to the sheer volume of the salt blocks that arrived downriver, it was quite possible that the land ahead was not very great. However, the Indian merchants who brought that salt to trade had informed the Indians at La Tora that the place where the salt was made was a great land, with enormous riches, ruled by an extremely powerful lord whose excellence and superiority was widely regarded. Jiménez was greatly dismayed that the path ahead of him was blocked, and that he would be unable to continue upriver; it seemed that any possibility of gathering more information about the source of the salt blocks was now lost.

Excerpt from a letter from Santa Marta's town council:
"Carta del cabildo de Santa Marta" (November 20,
1537), AGI Patronato 197, R. 13, fols. 59r–60r[22]

The following is an excerpt from a letter sent by the members of Santa Marta's town council to King Charles V. Dated November 20, 1537, the letter asks the king to name Jerónimo Lebrón Santa Marta's new permanent governor, officially replacing don Pedro Fernández de Lugo, who had passed away a year earlier; the letter also includes a plea for Crown support to launch another expedition into the interior (note that this is the only source in the chapter that makes any mention of Peru). Lebrón had been in Santa Marta for several months, having been sent as interim governor by the Audiencia of Santo Domingo in May 1537.[23]

22. A transcription of this letter can be found in Friede, *Documentos inéditos para la historia de Colombia*, 4:263–67.

23. A letter dated May 30, 1537, from the Audiencia of Santo Domingo explained that Lebrón had been sent one month earlier to Santa Marta to serve as interim governor until the king had the opportunity to appoint a permanent official. The same

By the time this letter was written, Jiménez de Quesada and his men had been in Muisca territory for more than nine months, but the only news of the expedition to reach Santa Marta had come from the men who had returned in the brigantines from La Tora in late 1536 or early 1537. And while several attempts were made to determine the fate of the Jiménez expedition, it was not until May 1539, when Jiménez and thirty of his men arrived in Cartagena (loaded with gold and emeralds from the conquest of Muisca territory) that Lebrón and the rest of Santa Marta's residents learned of the expedition's fate.

We, your very humble vassals and servants, members of the town council, judges and *regidores* of this city of Santa Marta, kiss Your Majesty's royal feet and hands. We write to inform you that roughly a year and a half ago, by Your Majesty's orders, don Pedro Fernández de Lugo came to this city as governor, bringing with him a certain number of people. On October 15 of last year, 1536, while serving as governor, it was our Lord God's will to carry don Pedro Fernández de Lugo from this present life. Afterward, we wrote to the officials in Your Majesty's royal *audiencia* in the city of Santo Domingo, informing them of the governor's death so that they might consider what action to take in order to best serve Your Majesty's interests. The president and judges of the *audiencia* considered it beneficial to send Jerónimo Lebrón to serve as governor of this city until the time when Your Majesty decrees how he might best be served.[24]

Jerónimo Lebrón arrived as governor roughly two months ago, and in that time that he has brought peace and justice to the city. From what we know of him, and from the loyalty he has demonstrated in every matter related to Your Majesty's service, we are most certain that from here on he will bring great benefits to Your Majesty and to the well-being of this town, which to this point he has done and is doing. We humbly implore Your Majesty to decree that he be named governor, because in doing so Your Majesty will be greatly served.

letter reported that the *audiencia* had heard rumors (no doubt from the men who had returned from La Tora) that the Jiménez expedition had found signs of Peru. See Carta de la Audiencia de Santo Domingo, AGI Santo Domingo 49, N. 55, R. 8, fols. 1v–2v.

24. Of course, under the terms of Pedro Fernández de Lugo's *capitulación*, Alonso Luis de Lugo was to inherit from his father the title of *adelantado*, as well as the governorship of Santa Marta.

Before don Pedro de Lugo passed away, he dispatched overland to Peru seventy horsemen and six hundred foot soldiers. He also sent seven ships by sea, which he and certain residents of Santa Marta equipped, to journey up the Río Grande and join those who went overland at a certain location where they had agreed to meet. It was our Lord God's will to send a terrible storm before the ships could enter the mouth of the Río Grande. Two vessels were lost, never again to appear; two others went to Cartagena, where they remained. Seeing the damage that this caused, the governor and several others equipped four more ships, which, together with the two that had remained from the last voyage, he ordered back up the Río Grande in pursuit of those who had gone by land. He also sent a caravel loaded with supplies; it was lost at the entrance to the river. The brigs sailed roughly two hundred and fifty leagues upriver until they caught up with the people who had gone overland. There, those who had come by land crossed the river to the other side, where they found a path that led up the mountains. They followed the path and discovered a land of vast plains, with a large Indian population. Seeing the excellent quality of the land, and taking with them news of the South Sea, and rumors of a rich and powerful *cacique* named Guazio, those who had climbed the sierra returned to the place where they had left the people from the brigs. There, the two groups reached an accord: the brigs would wait there for a period of six months, within which time those who went overland would return with all they had discovered.[25] Should they not return within six months, the brigs would wait two more months. By that point, the price of a horse among them had reached eight hundred pesos of fine gold. Having reached the agreement, those who went overland departed, very pleased and content; the brigs sailed downriver in search of provisions and whatever else was needed. They found themselves bartering for food fifty leagues downriver from the place where they had agreed to wait. The Indians with whom they were trading, seeing that all the people in the brigs were sick and wounded, launched an attack; they killed many people and took all the gold and much else, forcing the brigs to

---

25. Eighteen-year-old Gonzalo Hernández was one of the Spaniards who remained with the brigs. In Diego López de Castilblanco's 1558 *probanza*, Hernández testified that they had agreed to wait six months for Jiménez de Quesada and his men to return to the river. Hernández, however, claimed that the men in the brigs were attacked by Indians and were forced to return to Santa Marta before the six months expired. See servicios y méritos de Diego López de Castilblanco, AGI Patronato 158, N. 3, R. 4, fols. 647v–648r.

return to this city in order to recover and then return to comply with the agreement they had made with the others. The said agreement had been made on Christmas Day of last year 1536. By the time the brigs arrived in Santa Marta the *adelantado* already had passed away; and owing to the great hardships that the people of this city have endured, and continue to endure, two of the brigs have been lost because there was no way to refit them or carry out the necessary repairs.

Thus, there has not been any way to send assistance to the people who went overland, much of the blame for which can be assigned to the governor whom the *adelantado* left us in this city; he chose to do nothing about it.

The people who returned to Santa Marta in the brigs have stated and have testified in this city that those who went overland up the mountains had found signs of Peru. May it please our Lord God to guide this matter as best serves Him; and may Your Majesty, and all of us, be well rewarded.[26]

[fol. 60r] In the city of Santa Marta, November 20, 1537.[27]

Excerpt from the "Relación del Nuevo Reino: Letter from Captain Juan de San Martín and Captain Antonio de Lebrija" (July 8, 1539), AGI Patronato 27, R. 14. fols. 1r–1v[28]

The earliest firsthand account of the Jiménez expedition is a report written to King Charles V on July 8, 1539, by two of the expedition's

26. The letter did not end here. Instead, the members of Santa Marta's *cabildo* submitted three requests to the Crown. First, in order to attract more settlers to Santa Marta, and to encourage those already in the town to remain, they asked that for the next ten years the Crown exempt them from paying the *diezmo* on any gold found in the region. An exemption already existed for all gold mined in the region, but the *cabildo* wanted the exemption extended to all gold, no matter how or where it was obtained. Second, they requested that the Crown lift the ban on taking Indian slaves under the age of fourteen, claiming that the Spaniards should be permitted to capture Indians of any age, provided they were taken in legitimate warfare. And third, owing to the "terrible poverty" of Santa Marta's citizens and settlers (*vecinos y pobladores*), the members of the *cabildo* requested that the Crown lift its earlier provision that all of Santa Marta's inhabitants invest 10 percent of their wealth and belongings in the province. The end of the letter is signed Gonzalo [?], Juan Briceño, Luis de Esquivel, Diego [?], and Rodrigo [?] de Suárez.

27. The date November 29, 1537, appears on the back of the document.

28. For a complete Spanish transcription of this letter, see Tovar Pinzón, *Relaciones y visitas a los Andes*, vol. 3, *Región Centro-Oriental* (Bogotá: Colcultura, 1993), 93–117.

captains, Juan de San Martín and Antonio de Lebrija. Three years earlier, when the expedition departed from Santa Marta, San Martín was appointed as the expedition's chief accountant, while Lebrija was named its royal treasurer. This letter, which continues in Chapters 4 and 5 below, thus serves as their official report to the Crown. When Jiménez decided earlier that year to return to Spain to press his claims to Muisca territory before the Crown, Lebrija and San Martín were among the small group of Spaniards who accompanied him back to the coast. Thus the letter was written more than three years after the Jiménez expedition had initially set out from Santa Marta.

The following excerpt opens with a brief description of the origins of the expedition. It is worth noting that there is no mention of finding an overland route to Peru or of seeking the source of the Magdalena River. For captains San Martín and Lebrija, Pedro Fernández de Lugo dispatched the expedition into the interior because previous campaigns near Santa Marta had yielded few rewards.

It is already well known to Your Majesty that the *adelantado* don Pedro Fernández de Lugo came to the city and province of Santa Marta as your governor, and that he arrived there on January 2, 1536, with roughly eight hundred men. And Your Majesty will be aware from the letters from the province's previous governors, that Lugo launched several expeditions into the sierras of Santa Marta, from which he received great injury owing to the bellicose nature of the sierra's inhabitants.

Seeing that the people he had brought with him received few benefits from the sierras of Santa Marta, and instead suffered much damage and loss of life, on April 6 of the said year [1536], the *adelantado* sent his lieutenant, Gonzalo Jiménez, along with up to five hundred foot soldiers and horsemen, to follow the course of the Río Grande upriver. By sea, Lugo dispatched five brigantines, with all the men they could carry. And with them he sent us, royal officials who, on Your Majesty's behalf, reside in this province. Henceforth, we offer Your Majesty full notice and account of everything that has occurred on this expedition; given that we, along with *licenciado* Jiménez, are on our way to Spain to kiss Your Majesty's royal hands and provide a much longer account, Your Majesty will be well informed of this New Kingdom, recently conquered by *licenciado* Jiménez and all of Your Majesty's vassals who accompanied him.

Two of the brigs were lost at the mouth of the Río Grande, one
of which with everyone on board. The *adelantado* then refit another
two brigs, making five in total, with *licenciado* Gallegos serving
as lieutenant and captain, and he suffered great hardships in the
expedition up the Río Grande, until he passed beyond the point
where another group of Spaniards, previously sent by your governor Garcia de Lerma, had arrived.[29] The members of the expedition
always followed along the river's coast, by water and by land, but the
more they moved upriver, the fewer signs they saw of Indians and
good land. Nevertheless, Jiménez pushed forward with the expedition because he, and everyone else with him, had no intention of
turning around until they discovered land that would be of service to
Your Majesty. And through sheer persistence, crossing many rivers,
swamps, and difficult mountain passes, we arrived at a pueblo that
the Indians call La Tora; by that point, the majority of the people on
the expedition had died, both from hunger and because most were
newcomers from Spain.

Excerpt from the Anonymous "Relación de Santa Marta"
(c. 1545), AGI Patronato 27, R. 9, fols. 12r–13r[30]

The anonymous "Relación de Santa Marta" is a remarkably rich
source, both for the early history of Santa Marta and for the conquest of New Granada. It chronicles the history of the province of
Santa Marta from the earliest Spanish settlers to the year 1545. The
text is almost forty pages in length and therefore only the sections
related to the Jiménez expedition and the conquest of Muisca territory have been translated for this work.

While there is no clear evidence to indicate the identity of the
author of the Relación, it does appear to have been written by a
veteran of the Jiménez expedition. Not only that, but its style and
content follow a pattern similar to the *probanzas de méritos,* or
"proof-of-merit" petitions, so common during the early conquest
period. If in fact we read it as a *probanza,* the most likely author
would be Captain Antonio Díaz Cardoso, whose achievements and
contributions fill the account.

29. This is probably a reference to the settlement of Sompallón.
30. A complete transcription of the anonymous "Relación de Santa Marta" can be
found in Tovar Pinzón, *Relaciones y visitas a los Andes,* 2:125–88.

The first twelve folios of the anonymous Relación chronicle Santa Marta's early history; we pick up the story on folio 12, with don Pedro Fernández de Lugo's decision to send an expedition into the interior. The following excerpt offers one of the few accounts written from the perspective of the men who sailed up the Magdalena River in the brigantines.

With don Alonso [Luis de Lugo] having departed for Spain,[31] his father, the *adelantado,* decided to organize an expedition to march inland toward Quito; as his lieutenant and Captain General, Pedro de Lugo appointed *licenciado* Gonzalo Jiménez, whom the *adelantado* had brought from Spain as his lieutenant. Lugo decided to dispatch two separate armadas, one by land and the other by sea; for the land armada, Lugo sent his lieutenant Jiménez, and as captains, he sent Captain Juan de San Martín, Captain Juan de Céspedes, Captain Juan del Junco, Captain Lázaro Fonte, and Captain Gonzalo Suárez.[32]

By sea he dispatched don Diego de Cardona, Diego de Urbina, Captain Cardoso, a certain Orduña, and a certain Juan Chamorro;[33] those who went overland departed twenty-five days before those who went by sea. The latter set sail at the conclusion of the Holy

31. The circumstances of don Alonso's sudden, and unexpected, return to Spain remain unclear. In January 1536, shortly after the Lugo armada arrived in Santa Marta, Alonso set out with his father and roughly one thousand armed Spaniards, to pacify a region east of Santa Marta. After several military encounters in the valleys of Coto and Vallehermoso, an injured and fatigued don Pedro decided to return to Santa Marta, ordering his son to continue with the expedition. With his father gone, don Alonso led the eight hundred Spaniards who remained into the lands of the powerful *cacique* of Tairona. According to some accounts, in Tairona don Alonso collected more than three thousand pesos in gold and then, without informing his father and without dividing the spoils among his followers, secretly boarded a vessel in Santa Marta and returned to the Canary Islands. Don Alonso's actions led some chroniclers to condemn this supposed act of treachery. And while there were investigations of the matter, the Crown finally agreed in 1538 to absolve Alonso of any wrongdoing and, more important, to honor Alonso's claim to inherit his father's titles and possessions. In 1542 Alonso returned to Santa Marta to assume the governorship. For details of don Alonso Luis de Lugo's 1542 expedition from Santa Marta to Santa Fe, see José Ignacio Avellaneda Navas, *La expedición de Alonso Luis de Lugo al Nuevo Reino de Granada* (Bogotá: Banco de la República, 1994).

32. Here the author of the Relación fails to mention Captains Pedro Fernández de Valenzuela, Antonio de Lebrija, and Juan de Madrid.

33. Juan Chamorro was part of the small group of Spaniards ordered to remain in La Tora when Jiménez de Quesada and his men began their climb up the eastern highlands and into Muisca territory. On their return journey from La Tora to Santa Marta, Juan Chamarro and his nephew were killed in Indian attacks. See AGI Justicia 744, N. 2, bl. 3, fol. 55v.

Thursday procession. The brigs journeyed two leagues from Santa Marta, where they were to gather their crews. On Easter Saturday at 10:00, they set out from a town called Onxaca. From there, they had to sail another 8–10 leagues in order to reach the entrance to the Río Grande; but a terrible storm descended upon them, and they lost sight of one another. Everyone hurried abaft to seek shelter from the storm. Later, when the skies cleared, the ships were no longer all together, except for the *fusta* that carried don Diego de Cardona and Diego de Urbina, Captain Cardoso's brig, and another brig carrying a Flemish captain. They passed through the storm at the mouth of the river, but with the rough conditions and the thick fog they were unable to enter; therefore they sailed along the coast toward the town of Zanba, which is in the jurisdiction of the governorship of Cartagena. Having journeyed roughly eight leagues from the Río Grande toward Cartagena, the *fusta*'s rudder snapped, making it necessary to reach harbor. However, the *fusta* sank; and while the crew survived, everything else was lost. Captain Cardoso and the Flemish captain hurried to the harbor at the port of Zanba, in the governorship of Cartagena, where they anchored and took refuge from the storm. The following day they sailed on to Cartagena in order to gather all the necessary supplies; during the storm they had tossed everything into the sea, and they had nothing left but artillery. On their arrival in Cartagena, they found a certain Manjarres, who had been part of the same armada, and who, owing to the storm, also had sailed to Cartagena.[34] While they rested in Cartagena, Diego de Urbina and don Diego de Cardona arrived by land, with all of the soldiers they had brought with them.

From there, Captain Cardoso, together with two or three of his servants, returned to Santa Marta, leaving behind the soldiers he had brought in his company; they did not want to follow him back to Santa Marta.[35] And thus Captain Cardoso returned to Santa Marta to

34. One of the survivors, Francisco Menacho, claims that three of the five ships that left Santa Marta sank during the storm. Menacho survived the storm on one of two remaining ships, captained by Manjarres, which docked in Cartagena. Menacho did not join the next armada up the Magdalena River; instead, he eventually made his way to Peru, from where he submitted his *probanza* in 1561. See servicios y méritos de Francisco Menacho, AGI Patronato 154, N. 3, R. 2, fols. 636r–636v.

35. According to Pedro Garcia Ruíz, who testified in Ortún Velasco's *probanza* of 1564, some of the survivors decided not to return to Santa Marta, and instead made their way to Peru. See servicios y méritos de Ortún Velasco, AGI Patronato 152, N. 3, R. 1, fols. 254v–255r.

inform the *adelantado* what had happened to the armada; don Diego de Cardona and Diego de Urbina remained in Cartagena and did not wish to return to Santa Marta.

On his arrival in Santa Marta, Captain Cardoso discovered that, having received already the news that the ships had been lost, don Pedro de Lugo had organized another armada on which he planned to send *Licenciado* Gallegos as lieutenant and a certain Captain Albarrazín and Gómez de Corral as captains. Following his arrival in Santa Marta, Captain Cardoso embarked with the said armada in one of the brigs, recruiting people to take with him. They departed from Santa Marta and, with great difficulty, entered the Río Grande. They followed its course upriver in an effort to catch up with *licenciado* Jiménez and his men, who were traveling overland; eighty leagues upriver they caught up with them, and from there they all continued together, some by land and others by river. Almost eight months passed from their departure from Santa Marta until their arrival in La Tora, located roughly 100 leagues from the sea.

We endured a great many hardships on the journey from Cuatro Brazos (La Tora) to this new kingdom, as much from having to slash new paths through the mountains and hills, as from hunger and sickness. And we arrived in this kingdom naked and barefoot, burdened by the weight of our own weapons, all of which caused the deaths of large numbers of Spaniards. In fact, so many died that by the time we reached this kingdom, we were no more than 165 Spaniards.

4

Into the Highlands: From La Tora to Muisca Territory

For almost three months, Jiménez and his men remained in La Tora, waiting for the rains to subside.[1] The break was also supposed to give the sick and the injured much-needed time to recover. It did not. When the expedition finally left La Tora in late December 1536, another two hundred Spaniards had lost their lives, most from malnutrition, starvation, and disease.[2]

Unfortunately, few details remain from this phase of the expedition; the expedition's official logbook did not record a single entry from their stay at La Tora, and the scattered accounts from veterans of the expedition present a confusing and at times contradictory chronology of events. Nonetheless, it appears that events unfolded in the following manner.

With the sick and injured recovering in La Tora, Jiménez ordered a series of small expeditionary forces to explore the surrounding region, gather food and other provisions, and search for signs of rich new lands. Most returned with similar reports of unpopulated lands, no gold, and nothing but water, flooded plains, and unreachable distant mountain ranges. Jiménez and his captains convened to discuss the next course of action. With the food supply dwindling and the mortality rate on the rise, they agreed to send out one last expeditionary force, led by Captain Juan de San Martín.

In his lengthy *probanza de mérito* (proof-of-merit petition) from 1565, Bartolomé Camacho recorded his recollections of the San Martín expedition. According to Camacho, conditions in La Tora were unbearable; the men survived by eating snakes, lizards, and other assorted vermin. Camacho claimed that at one point all the captains gathered in conference and agreed to send Captain San Martín on

1. The epigraph is from servicios y méritos de Diego Romero, AGI Patronato 154, N. 3, R. 1, fol. 504r. Of course, the 165 survivors whom Romero cites in his *probanza* is not an accurate figure; at least 179 Spaniards, as well as an unknown number of slaves and native carriers, survived the expedition.
2. Avellaneda Navas, *Conquerors of the New Kingdom of Granada,* 34.

one last reconnaissance effort; if it failed, the entire expedition agreed to abandon the quest and return to Santa Marta.

With two canoes and a force of no more than twenty, San Martín and his men paddled upriver forty leagues from La Tora.[3] From there they turned east to follow a tributary that descended from the eastern highlands, hoping that it would reveal a route into the mountains. After a lengthy exploration, their search proved unsuccessful. Dejected at finding no clear path into the mountains and no sign of riches, San Martín decided to turn back to La Tora. At that moment, overwhelmed by his "strong desire to serve Your Majesty," Camacho jumped into the river and swam across to the other bank. There he captured some Indians and discovered several storehouses filled with large salt blocks and rich cotton *mantas;* this fortuitous discovery, Camacho boasted, led directly to the conquest of the New Kingdom of Granada.[4]

Whether or not we accept Camacho's exaggerated rendering of these events, all accounts seem to agree that the discovery of mined salt and elaborately woven cotton cloth altered the expedition's fate. According to Captain Juan de Céspedes, who had remained in La Tora when Captain San Martín and his men set out, news of the discovery of salt and cotton *mantas* filled the entire camp with a great desire to continue the expedition.[5]

Still, Jiménez and his men were faced with a difficult choice. On the one hand, they could return to Santa Marta to gather reinforcements and more provisions, and report their findings to Governor Lugo (they were unaware that Lugo recently had passed away). On the

3. Readers will note that in Captain San Martín and Captain Lebrija's letter that appears in this chapter, they stated that the distance was twenty-five leagues, as opposed to the forty leagues recorded in Camacho's *probanza.*

4. Of course, none of the witnesses who testified in Camacho's *probanza* attributed the discovery and conquest of New Granada solely to Camacho's actions. But neither did they deny the significance of the discovery of the salt and *mantas.* They simply told the story differently; for example, one of Camacho's witnesses, Juan Rodríguez Parra, testified that he had joined Camacho in crossing the river and that together they discovered two Indian houses (*bohíos*) that contained the salt and *mantas.* Rodríguez also suggested that had he and Camacho not made this discovery, the entire expedition would have turned back to Santa Marta and the New Kingdom of Granada would not have been conquered. See servicios y méritos de Bartolomé Camacho, AGI Patronato 157, N. 1, R. 2, fol. 81r, and AGI Patronato 160 N. 1, R. 6. For Juan Rodríguez Parra's testimony, see AGI Patronato 157 N. 1, R. 2, fols. 153r–153v.

5. See servicios de méritos de Juan Ramírez de la Hinojosa, AGI Patronato 158, N. 3, R. 1, fol. 395r.

other hand, they could shift their attention away from the exploration of the Magdalena River and try to locate the source of the salt and cotton *mantas* somewhere up in the eastern highlands. With virtually no treasure to show for their eight-month expedition, it is hardly surprising that Jiménez and his captains agreed to press forward.

At this stage Jiménez decided to lead another expedition to verify Captain San Martín's claims and explore the route into the highlands. Somewhere near the base of the Opón Mountains, however, Jiménez fell ill. Unable to continue, he ordered Captain Juan de Céspedes and Captain Antonio de Lebrija to lead a small force to search for a route over the mountains. According to Céspedes, it took twenty days to cross the sierra; after capturing several native guides, who helped guide them across the mountains, they saw evidence of rich new lands and dense settlements.

When Jiménez learned of their discovery he ordered the entire force to return to La Tora. There, he and his captains selected two hundred of the strongest and healthiest men, ordering the rest to stay behind with the brigantines. The men who remained in La Tora promised to wait six months for Jiménez and the others to return; if they received no word within that six-month period, they were to return to Santa Marta. However, it was not long before that promise was broken.

Soon after the two forces separated, the men in the brigantines set out to explore on their own; they sailed thirty leagues downriver, at which point they were attacked by local natives. According to one of the men present, Gonzalo Hernández, the small Spanish force, made up of sick and injured men, could not repel the attack; therefore, he claimed, they had no choice but to return to Santa Marta.[6] Another survivor, Juan Castellanos, testified that the intense fighting continued over the course of two days and two nights, and that at least thirty Spaniards were either injured or killed. The brigantines' commander, *Licenciado* Diego Hernández Gallego, was among the injured, having been struck in the face by an arrow.[7] Nonetheless, in early 1537 Gallego and a handful of survivors made it back to Santa Marta; more than two years would pass before they learned the fate of their colleagues who followed Jiménez into the eastern highlands.

6. Testimony of Gonzalo Hernández, servicios y méritos de Diego López de Castilblanco, AGI Patronato 158, N. 3, R. 4, fols. 647v–648r.

7. AGI Justicia 744, N. 2, bl. 3, fol. 51v.

Jiménez and two hundred of his men left La Tora on December 28, 1536, to begin the long climb up and across the Opón Mountains.[8] This stage of the expedition took more than two months, over which time another twenty Spaniards died.[9] At last, in early March 1537, eleven months after the expedition had departed from Santa Marta, Jiménez's force of 179 Spaniards (and an unknown number of slaves, native guides, and carriers) successfully crossed the Opón Mountains and arrived in the Grita Valley, land of the Muisca.

The following accounts follow the Jiménez expedition over the eight- or nine-month period from the arrival in La Tora through the early stages of the conquest of Muisca territory. The first two documents, namely, the letter from captains San Martín and Lebrija, and the anonymous Relación, both outline events from October 1536 until July 1537. By contrast, the third account, a lengthy excerpt from the "Epítome de la conquista del Nuevo Reino de Granada," may seem somewhat out of place. Instead of recording the history of the expedition from La Tora to Muisca territory, the following segment of the Epítome provides some of the richest descriptions of Muisca society and culture that we have.

Excerpt from the "Relación del Nuevo Reino: Letter from Captain Juan de San Martín and Captain Antonio de Lebrija" (July 8, 1539), AGI Patronato 27, R. 14, fols. 1v–3v

This brief excerpt picks up the letter where it left off at the end of Chapter 3. Here, San Martín and Lebrija briefly chronicle the expedition's crossing of the Opón Mountains and into Muisca territory. The letter offers few specific details of the six- or seven-month period it covers, but it is worth noting how the two captains portray the Muisca leader Bogotá and the Panches, and the emphasis they place on the emerald mines.

While camped in La Tora, which we think is located roughly two hundred leagues from the sea, lieutenant (Jiménez) witnessed the dreadful nature of the surrounding lands; as each day passed, the river revealed fewer and fewer settlements. Twice he ordered certain brigantines ahead to explore. However, upon their return they spoke

8. Friede, *Descubrimiento del Nuevo Reino de Granada*, 61.
9. See Avellaneda Navas, *Expedición de Gonzalo Jiménez de Quesada*, 24.

only of worse conditions, of land on which it was nearly impossible even to walk on account that the river had flooded everything. In recognition of the wretched quality of the lands ahead, Jiménez decided to determine if it were possible to reach the sierra that extends along the Río Grande, roughly twenty leagues away from the river. To that point they had not been able to reach it because the land between the mountains and the river is completely flooded, and full of lagoons. In order to carry out the exploration of the sierra, Jiménez sent Captain Juan de San Martín, who with some men took several canoes up a branch of a river that descended from the mountains. On his return, San Martín stated that he made it about twenty-five leagues from where he departed and that he discovered some evidence of human settlements; and although the settlements were small, they were located along the route on which the salt from the highlands was carried down to trade along the river. Seeing this, Jiménez determined to go there himself, taking with him the best and healthiest people then available, to see what lay ahead. He departed from La Tora, leaving the camp behind, and he journeyed until he arrived at the place San Martín earlier had reached. There, owing to his poor health, he remained, ordering Captain Antonio de Lebrija and Captain Juan de Céspedes to venture ahead. With up to twenty-five men, the two captains departed to find out what they might discover in the mountains.[10] They crossed over twenty-five leagues of rough mountainous terrain until they reached a flat and open land where they saw evidence of fertile soil and dense settlements. With that news they returned to where they had left Jiménez, and from there they all returned to camp at La Tora to gather the men and proceed toward the newly discovered land. Already a large portion of the people who had remained in camp had died from the causes listed above; Jiménez departed with the strongest and healthiest people, ordering that all the infirm return to the brigantines.[11]

Marching along on the campaign, Jiménez crossed the high mountain range they call Opón, and exited into the open plains that the first discoverers had seen earlier. There, Jiménez initiated the

10. In his 1571 *probanza*, Juan Ramírez de la Hinojosa testified that he was one of the twenty-five men who joined Captain Lebrija.

11. We do not know precisely how many Spaniards returned to Santa Marta in the brigantines; Antonio Díaz Cardoso testified in 1562 that as many as fifty or sixty men remained behind. See servicios y méritos de Francisco Figueredo, AGI Patronato 155, N. 1, R. 8, fol. 429r.

conquest of this New Kingdom. Taking stock of the people he had brought with him, Jiménez discovered that in total we were no more than 170 foot soldiers and horsemen who had managed to make it this far;[12] everyone else had died along the way, or had returned in the brigantines to Santa Marta, very ill.[13]

Seeing the excellent nature of the land, and how the Indians always brought us salt, which they packed into large blocks, Jiménez decided to try to seek its source. And because we had no translators in this land, he decided to use sign language to ask where the salt was made. And thus the Indians led us to the place where they made the salt, which came from a body of salt water. In the fourteen or fifteen days since we entered these open plains, we passed through many large settlements, with abundant foodstuffs; and in many places they made this salt, which is white and very tasty.

Having arrived at these "salt towns," already the land showed clear signs of what it offered, and of what would be found ahead, with fertile soils and large numbers of Indians; and the nature of the houses they built differed from anything we had found up to that point. In particular, one day's journey from the salt town, we entered the territory of the most important lord in all the land; they call him Bogotá. And his status was clearly manifested in one of the private residences that we encountered; and even though it was built of thatch, it could still be considered one of the finest houses ever seen in the Indies. To that point, in all the towns through which we

12. The precise number of horses that reached the New Kingdom is unclear, but it was perhaps somewhere between eighty and one hundred. However, we know that before the general distribution of the booty, the Spaniards awarded a total of 2,500 pesos of fine gold as compensation to the nineteen individuals who lost one or more horses over the course of the expedition. It appears that hunger led some Spaniards to kill and eat their horses. See servicios y méritos de Pedro de Sotelo, AGI Patronato 156, R. 11, fol. 1164r. In total, at least twenty-one stallions and five mares died between the time of the expedition's departure in April 1536 and the distribution of the booty in June 1538. See AGI Escribanía 1006A, Cuaderno 5, fols. 9v–10r.

13. We do not know the exact number of people who returned from La Tora to Santa Marta, but several veterans of the expedition testified that as many as thirty Spaniards made it back to the coast. There may have been as many as fifty when the brigantines left La Tora, but some Spaniards, including Juan Chamorro and his nephew, lost their lives on the return voyage. See the testimonies of Juan López and Pedro García Ruíz, servicios y méritos de Diego Montañez, AGI Patronato 163, R. 1, fols. 34v, 41r. Juan de Castellanos testified that thirty Spaniards were either injured or killed by natives on the return to Santa Marta. See AGI Justicia 744, N. 2, bl. 3, fols. 51r–55v.

had passed, we saw signs of some gold and emeralds. And given that Bogotá chose to resist our entry into his land, he dispatched a reasonable number of Indians, who came at us from our rearguard position. However, this proved to little avail because in the end, as they are Indians, they turned tail, and we inflicted some damage on them.

This Bogotá is the most important lord in this land because many other principal lords are his subjects; it is rumored that he is extremely rich because the natives of this land claim that he has a house of gold and a great number of very precious emeralds. His vassals pay him far too many honors because the truth of the matter is that the lords of this New Kingdom keep their Indian subjects under tight control. Bogotá has conquered and tyrannized a great part of this land; to this point we have received nothing from him because he has fled, together with many other leaders and all of his gold, to a steep and craggy mountain, where no harm can come to him without a great amount of effort from Spaniards.

Having arrived in Bogotá's realm, Jiménez sent out two expeditions in two separate directions; the first led by Captain Juan de Céspedes and the second by Captain Juan de San Martín. Both returned with the news that they had come across a nation of people called Panches, whose territory surrounds this area and the greater part of the Valley of Bogotá because there is nothing separating the two regions but a small mountain range.[14] The Panches use different weapons than the people of Bogotá, and the two are fierce enemies.

Already by this point our interpreters were casting light on more and more matters. And we were beginning to understand each other better and better, so much so that some Indians brought us gold and [emeralds], knowing that we held both in great esteem. And they did this in spite of the fact that they valued emeralds even more than gold, and they told us that they would guide us to where the emeralds were extracted from below the ground. Hearing this, Jiménez

14. Unfortunately, beyond the vague references from documents translated in this volume, we know very little about the Panches. While they appear to have resided somewhere to the southwest of Muisca territory, toward the Magdalena River, we do not know the precise boundaries of Panche territory. Nor do we understand the nature of the conflict between the Panches and the Muiscas. For a brief description of the Panches, see Avellaneda Navas, *Conquerors of the New Kingdom of Granada,* 114.

ordered the camp out of the Valley of Bogotá, to search for the emerald mines. They arrived at a valley, that they later named the Valley
of the Trumpet, where Jiménez ordered Captain Pedro de Valenzuela
out to discover the emerald mines.[15] Valenzuela departed with several
others, and after six days they arrived at the said mines, where he and
the other Spaniards with him, watched the Indians extract the emeralds from below the ground, and they witnessed such strange new
things. The mines are located roughly fifteen leagues from the Valley
of the Trumpet, in a very high and sparse mountain range. It appears
that the emeralds are extracted from an area about one league in
size. The lord of the mines is a very principal Indian by the name of
Somyndoco.[16] He is sovereign over many vassals and settlements,
and his private residence is located three leagues' distance from the
mines. No other Indians but his subjects work the mines, and only
at certain times of the year, accompanied by many ceremonies. After
the emeralds are extracted, they are traded and exchanged among the
Indians. The main items of barter are the gold beads that are made in
this land, as well as clothing, much of which is made from cotton.

Those who went on the discovery of the emerald mines said that
from the mines they could see some great plains [*llanos*], so marvelous that nothing like them ever had been seen. On hearing this news,
Jiménez moved the camp closer to the mines, not only to become
better informed about the mines themselves, but also to see if it were
possible to reach the *llanos*. From there he dispatched Captain Juan
de San Martín to discover the *llanos*, because from what was said of
them, they appeared to be populated. But the journey proved so difficult that they could find no access from any direction, either because
of the steepness of the terrain or on account of the great rivers that
descended into the *llanos*. For those reasons it was not possible to
reach the *llanos*, and therefore they left it at that.

15. It appears that Jiménez sent Captain Valenzuela out to explore the emerald
mines in late May or early June 1538. According to the anonymous "Relación de
Santa Marta," (see Chapter 5), Valenzuela's return journey took fifteen days. The
expedition's official logbook recorded that Valenzuela returned from the mines on
June 14; and he did not return empty-handed. The book shows that the captain and
his men brought with them 518 pesos of fine gold, 168 pesos of low-grade gold, and
seventy-two emeralds, all of which was added to the overall booty acquired during the
conquest. See AGI Escribanía 1006A, Cuaderno 5, fol. 6v.

16. Somondoco.

Excerpt from the Anonymous "Relación de Santa Marta"
(c. 1545), AGI Patronato 27, R. 9, fols. 12v–13v[17]

Once again, the following excerpt from the anonymous Relación picks up from the selection translated in Chapter 3. As with the previous document, this section of the Relación covers the period from the departure from La Tora in late 1536, to Captain Fernández de Valenzuela's expedition to discover the emerald mines in June 1537.

And there they remained in La Tora for more than three months, searching for a path they could follow into the mountains; but the land between the Río Grande and the mountains was dominated by large lagoons, filled with islands, and dense forests. Captain Cardoso and Captain Albarrazín ventured out in search of some route. At last, they discovered a river that came down from the mountains; they paddled upstream by canoe and found evidence of paths used by Indians to travel up and down the sierra. The two captains returned to camp to share the news of their discovery; and it seemed to them that they could take their horses up that way into the mountains. Therefore, the entire camp agreed to send Captain San Martín inland to discover more about this land. Captain San Martin departed, and was gone for fifteen or twenty days. He found that the Indians went there in search of salt. On seeing evidence of large numbers of people, San Martín returned to camp because he had few Spaniards with him. Jiménez immediately dispatched Captain Céspedes and Captain Lebrija, together with some men, to discover what was farther ahead.[18] They departed; and over the first three, four, and five days, they found nothing but uninhabited wilderness. Therefore, they turned back toward camp after they came across populated settlements, which they had spotted from the peaks of some hills they had

17. In the margin it reads, "Here begins the year 1534." However, the date is incorrect; it should read 1537.

18. As a witness in Captain Juan de Céspedes's *probanza de mérito,* Gonzalo Jiménez de Quesada testified that he sent Captain Céspedes, Captain Lebrija, and some men to explore the Sierra de Opón, and that the men returned to camp with reports of open plains that could be seen from the top of the mountain. What they saw, reported Jiménez, was the frontier of the New Kingdom of Granada. See servicios y méritos de Juan de Céspedes, AGI Patronato 160, N. 3, R. 3, fols. 1184r–1184v. Another witness in the same *probanza,* Alonso Domínguez Beltrán, added that Céspedes and Lebrija also captured some native guides to lead them over the mountains. Ibid., fol. 1179r.

climbed. On their return to camp they shared the news of what they had witnessed in that land; they had seen much smoke, a sign of a large population.

On hearing this news, Jiménez and the captains met, and they decided that the people in the brigs should return to Santa Marta with all the infirm; or alternatively, they should wait at the river until the others had the opportunity to explore the land further and discover what it contained. And for the journey, on account of his vast experience and his knowledge of the land, they called on Captain Cardoso to leave his post on the brigs and accompany them. And because he was an expert in the mountains, they also brought Captain Albarrazín. Together with the camp, they crossed great mountains and vast uninhabited lands, suffering such hunger that they were forced to eat a leather shield, as well as some mangy, crippled dogs. And thus they continued their journey, enduring much hardship, until they made it out of the mountains and into open plains. There they began to find great quantities of food, of maize and other agricultural products, as well as deer and many other sources of animal meat. There is a great abundance of *curíes* (guinea pigs). For three or four days they roamed around the valley. On the following morning, because they were all weary, they decided to make their way to a town that they had spotted from the mountains. The Indians watched as everyone proceeded toward town, leaving no one in the rear guard but Captain Cardoso, four or five horsemen, and many sick and injured on horseback. Seeing this, the Indians attacked and killed many of the Christians in the rear guard, which we know because Captain Cardoso later was rescued by those who were up ahead.

That night the Spaniards lodged in that town; and the next day they continued ahead two leagues, where they came across a brand-new settlement, recently built by a great lord named Bogotá. The town was quite splendid; the few houses were very large, and made of finely worked thatch. The houses were well fenced, with walls made from cane stalks, elegantly crafted. Each house had ten or twelve doors, with twisting and turning walls to protect each entrance. Two walls enclosed the entire town, and between them was a great plaza. And between the inner wall and the houses was another beautiful plaza. One of the houses was filled with dried venison, cured without salt.

Having arrived in that town, they decided to lodge there because they found that no one was opposed to their presence. They remained there that entire day. On the following day, ten or twelve Indians arrived, each wearing black *mantas* and carefully knit black cotton hats. They brought the Spaniards some venison on behalf of the lord (Bogotá), as well as a little gold. They claimed that they had come to pay honor to those Spaniards they had killed in battle; and they began to sing, in a manner similar to a wail. However, because they did not have any translators, the Christians did not understand the songs. The wails and shrieks continued for an hour and a half, at which point the Indians departed. A message was sent with them to tell their *cacique* to come forward and make friends with the Christians. If he did not, the Christians would raze the town to the ground, and wage war against those who chose not to come in peace.

On another day, the camp departed from that town and traveled two leagues away to another town, called Chía, which means Prince.[19] The town carries this name because in it resides Chía, the successor to the lord Bogotá. And so they arrived in Chía, which they found abandoned; all the Indian men and women had gone. The Christians remained there for a couple of days. Perhaps out of fear or in an effort to learn more about the Spaniards, several Indian *caciques* sent the Christians food and *mantas*; they did this in spite of the fact that they were Bogotá's subjects. When the lord Bogotá learned of this, he ordered Chía and his captains to kill anyone who brought food or cotton *mantas* to the Christians; they obeyed, and many Indians were beaten with clubs, and their food taken. Others had their *mantas* ripped into pieces, and the shreds tied around their necks, a sign of great dishonor. Those punished were told, "go and run to those Christians and ask them to come seek vengeance on your behalf"; and thus some Indians came to the Christians to complain.

Seeing this, the Christians decided to dispatch Captain Cardoso, together with four horsemen and up to twenty-five foot soldiers; they could not send more on account that so many Spaniards had fallen ill or were too exhausted. Cardoso and his men departed. They prepared an ambush at the base of the mountain, beside a river,

19. In the Chibcha language spoken by the Muiscas, the term *chía* (or *chíe*) meant "moon," or "light." See María Stella González de Pérez, *Diccionario y gramática Chibcha: Manuscrito anónimo de la Biblioteca Nacional de Colombia* (Bogotá: Instituto Caro y Cuervo, 1987), 275 and 341.

where most of the Indians were gathered. There they waited until
daybreak; and when they saw the sentries retire, they attacked the
guards from behind, and together they entered the camp. Having
been taken by complete surprise, the Indians were too disheartened
to mount any defense; instead, they began to flee. The Christians
captured a great many women and children, choosing not to chase
after those they had watched flee. Instead, the Christians fired shots
into the air, calling all the people from the camp to gather in order to
carry the spoils back to camp. The prize consisted of the souls of up
to three hundred women and children, whose services helped to compensate many Spaniards who enjoyed no help whatsoever, and who
barely could afford clothing. They took from there a great number of
emeralds, many cotton *mantas*, and many other things to supply the
camp. With these spoils, Captain Cardoso returned to camp, where
he was received with great cheer. After his arrival, as many as twenty
Indians appeared, among them ten whom Captain Cardoso had set
free, with the charge of taking a message to Chía, requesting that he
come forward and make peace with the Christians. If he did, then the
Christians would return all the women and children they had taken.
And it was with that purpose in mind that the twenty Indians had
come to camp to negotiate; however, the negotiations failed because
they were unable to convince the Chía to come forward and appear in
person. Therefore Jiménez divided all the spoils among the captains
and the soldiers as he best saw fit. Everyone worked to teach Spanish
to the Indian women so that they could understand one another; and
the women learned it quickly.

They had been in that town for a few days when they heard
rumors that the great *cacique* Bogotá was three leagues away from
Chía, in a town called Bogotá. The Christians thus made their way
to Bogotá, but when they arrived they found not a single Indian. As
they walked around the area, a *cacique* by the name of Suba Usac
[Suba Usaque] came out to meet them.[20] He brought meat and other

20. Later in this account (see Chapter 5), the author of the Relación once again
returns to Suba Usaque, whom he identifies as both a *cacique* (chief) and as the uncle
of the most powerful ruler in the region, the Bogotá. If we are to believe the Relación,
Suba Usaque allied himself with the Spaniards, offering them food and clothing. It
is unclear why Suba Usaque turned against his son-in-law, but the decision cost him
dearly, as an angry Bogotá had his uncle arrested, his houses burned, and some of his
followers executed.

things, but at the time the Christians did not realize what a powerful lord he was. Consequently, they let him go free. Afterward, he
became a great friend and ally to the Christians, always sending them
meat and *mantas;* however, he remained in hiding for fear of Bogotá.

While camped in this town they call Bogotá, the Christians dispatched many messengers to the *cacique* Bogotá, asking that he come
forward to make peace; however, Bogotá never desired to do that.
Hearing that the *cacique* could be found three leagues away, Jiménez
decided to send some men out to search for him; he ordered Captain San Martín and Captain Céspedes to lead the expedition. They
were unable to locate Bogotá; but they returned with more than two
hundred Indian men and women they had found in a nearby town.
The other Indians had withdrawn into the mountains. Many Indians
come to this town, bringing the Christians gold, emeralds and *mantas.* At night, some Indians have a habit of setting the thatch houses
on fire in an attempt to burn the Christians to death. They have done
this on three or four occasions, and the Christians are very cautious
of it happening again. And with matters thus, several Indians came
to the Christians and offered to take them to the place where the
emeralds were mined. They added that the Indians there possessed
such great quantities of emeralds that they would give them over by
the handful. But they said all of this simply to get the Christians out
of their territory and into the lands of Tunja, who was their enemy.
Seeing that the Indians from Bogotá were growing in strength, the
Christians decided to go there. After a few days' march with their
guides, they arrived at the town of the *cacique* of Turmequé; there,
some Indians brought them a few emeralds and some gold, but in
very small quantities. Therefore, the Christians decided to have their
guides lead them directly to the emerald mines; and they sent Captain Pedro Fernández de Valenzuela, among certain others. The return
journey took fifteen days, and Christians and Indians alike dug
around in those mines. Together they were unable to extract more
than just one or two emeralds because they are extremely difficult to
mine. These mines are in the mountains, the highest mountains in
all that land; they are so high that from the top the flat plains below
look like the sea.

These emerald mines are in the ground, and the soil contains certain sticky, clay veins, which turn the color of sky blue. Inside these
veins the emeralds grow. They are all born so perfectly eight-sided,

that no lapidary could carve them better. The emeralds emerge white in color, but over time they turn increasingly green, because some are found that are half white and half green. Many of the emeralds are found together in clusters, shooting out like little branches from vines that grow out of trunks of slate. Other emeralds are found in isolation.

Excerpt from the "Epítome de la conquista del Nuevo Reino de Granada," fols. 3–7

Once again the Epítome offers few details about the expedition itself. Apart from a brief description of the Opón Mountains, the account that follows says little about the conquest itself. Nor does it follow any concise chronology. Instead, this lengthy excerpt from the Epítome offers some of the earliest and richest descriptions of Muisca culture, including descriptions of weapons and warfare, religion, marriage practices, law and government, and architecture and diet.

As previously mentioned, Jiménez decided to follow a small tributary up into the Opón Mountains, and thus he moved inland, leaving the Río Grande behind. The brigs returned to the sea. However, most of the crew, and the brigs' captains remained with Jiménez, as partial replacements for the large numbers of Jiménez's men who had died on the expedition. Jiménez spent many days in the discovery of the Opón Mountains, which extend fifty leagues, across rough, mountainous terrain, sparsely populated by Indians. It was with enormous difficulty that Jiménez crossed them. In all the small towns through which he passed in those mountains, he always came across great quantities of the aforementioned salt. It seemed apparent to Jiménez that this was the road on which the salt was carried down from the mountains for trade along the Río Grande. After overcoming a great many obstacles, *licenciado* Jiménez made it across those mountains and happened upon a flat, open plain. This is the New Kingdom of Granada, which begins just beyond those said mountains. When the Spaniards set their eyes on that land, it appeared to them that they had reached their desired destination. Therefore, they set out to conquer it. However, they did so blindly because they knew nothing at all about the land in which they found themselves. Moreover, there were no interpreters who could communicate with the Indians from the New Kingdom because the language spoken by the Indians along the Río Grande is not spoken by the Indians in the mountains, nor is the language in the New Kingdom the same as that spoken in the mountains. Nevertheless, as best they possibly could, over the course of the exploration and conquest of the new Kingdom of Granada, the Spaniards began to acquire information and knowledge about the region. And everything unfolded in the following manner.

One might say with some certainty that this New Kingdom of Granada, which begins just beyond the Opón Mountains, is completely flat and densely populated. Its inhabitants are settled in valleys, with each valley supporting its own population. These plains and the entire New Kingdom are surrounded and enclosed by mountains and hills, which are inhabited by a certain group of Indians, called Panches. These Panches consume human flesh, and they are different from those in the New Kingdom, who do not. The climate in Panche territory also is different; it is a torrid zone, whereas the New Kingdom boasts a frigid climate, or at least a temperate one.[21] And just as that group of Indians carries the name Panches, the Indians from the New Kingdom are a different people and thus have a different name; they are called Moxcas [Muiscas].[22] This New Kingdom is 130 leagues in length more or less, and perhaps 30 wide; however, in some places it narrows to just 20 or even less. Most of the region is found five degrees from the Equinoctial line, although some of it falls at four, and still other parts are at three. This New Kingdom is divided into two parts, or rather, two provinces. One is called Bogotá, while the other is called Tunja; and the lords of [these

21. The average annual temperature in the region is 14°C, and there are no dramatic temperature variations over the course of the entire year. See Doris Kurella, "The Muisca: Chiefdoms in Transition," in *Chiefdoms and Chieftaincy in the Americas*, ed. Elsa M. Redmond (Gainesville: University Press of Florida), 192.

22. The term *Moxca*, or *Muisca*, comes from the Chibcha word for "man." In his lengthy chronicle of the conquest and colonization of New Granada, the seventeenth-century chronicler Pedro Simón related the origin of the term as a label to describe the region's inhabitants; Simón suggested that when the Spaniards first arrived in the eastern highlands, they asked a group of natives if the land was densely populated. The natives were said to have responded, "muexca bien agen," or "indeed, there are many of us." See Simón, *Noticias historiales de las conquistas*, 159. And while none of the participants in the Jiménez expedition confirms the accuracy of Simón's explanation, the term *muisca* does appear to have meant "man" or "person" (masculine); for example, a colonial Spanish-Chibcha catechism translates the Spanish word *hombre* (man) as *muysca*. See González de Pérez, *Diccionario y gramática Chibcha*, 339.

respective provinces] adopt these titles as their surnames. Both lords are extremely powerful, and each one rules over other great lords and *caciques*. The province of Bogotá is larger, and its lord more powerful than Tunja; in my opinion, the lord of Bogotá is capable of sending sixty thousand men, more or less, into battle. And here I offer a conservative estimate; others would suggest a much higher number. The lord Tunja is able to send forty thousand; but again, this figure likely is conservative and it does not conform to the opinion of others. These lords and the people of both provinces always have had their differences. Thus, from time immemorial the Indians from Bogotá and those from Tunja have been engaged in constant warfare, especially those from Bogotá. The reason for that is because they also fight against the Panches, who are much closer to Bogotá than they are to Tunja. As we already have mentioned, the Panches have the province of Bogotá surrounded.

The soil in Tunja is richer than the land in Bogotá, although the latter also is highly productive. And the best gold and precious emerald stones are always found in Tunja. The riches taken from both provinces were bountiful indeed; however, they did not begin to compare to the riches discovered in Peru. Nonetheless, as far as emeralds are concerned, far greater quantities were found in this New Kingdom than were discovered during the conquest of Peru; not only that, but it has been said that never, since the creation of the world, have so many been found in one place. When it came time to divide the shares among the soldiers after the conquest was completed, they distributed among themselves more than seven thousand emeralds, including some very rich stones of great value. And this is one of the reasons why the discovery of this New Kingdom must be considered the greatest thing to have happened in all the Indies; we know of no other Christian Prince, nor infidel, who possesses what has been discovered in this New Kingdom, and this in spite of the fact that for so long the Indians tried to keep the location of the mines a secret. And we know of no other mines anywhere in the world that are equal to these mines, even though we are aware that such mines must exist because there are precious stones elsewhere. Some emeralds have been found in Peru, but the location of the mines never has been determined. In this New Kingdom, the mines are located in the province of Tunja, and it is quite something to see where God felt himself served to place those mines. They are in a strange land, at one end of a barren mountain range. This treeless sierra is surrounded by other, densely forested mountains, which form a kind of pathway through which to enter into the mining zone. The entire region is made up of extremely rough terrain. From one end of the mines to the other is a distance of just half a league, or even less. In order to extract the emeralds, the Indians have constructed certain devices, which consist of large, wide irrigation channels, through which water passes in order to wash away the earth and thus expose the veins where the emeralds are located. For that reason, they only work the mines at a certain time of year, which is during the rainy season. This enables them to move great quantities of earth, thus allowing them to follow the exposed veins. The soil at those mines is loose, easily movable, and very porous, and it remains thus until the Indians come across one of the veins, which is made up of a clay-like substance. The Indian miners then follow the vein, and with their wooden tools they remove the emeralds that they discover within it. In this practice, as in so many others, the Indians perform all kinds of sorcery to help them find the emeralds. They drink and eat certain herbs, after which they reveal in which veins the miners will unearth the finest stones. The lord of these mines is a *cacique* named Sumindoco,[23] a subject of the great *cacique* of Tunja. And Sumindoco's land and the mines are located in the furthest reaches of the province of Tunja.

As far as the conquest itself is concerned, when the Christians entered that New Kingdom, the native people received them with great fear; in fact, so great was their fear that they believed that the Christians were children of the sun and the moon, whom these Indians worshipped. The Indians claim that, as man and wife, the sun and the moon have sexual relations and that the Christians were their offspring, whom the sun and moon sent from the sky in order to punish the Indians for their sins. For that reason, they called the Spaniards *uchies*, a term composed from the word *usa*, which in their language means "sun," and the word *chia*, which means moon. Put together, the term means children of the sun and moon. Thus, when the Christians entered into the first towns of the New Kingdom, the inhabitants abandoned their settlements, and climbed to the top of the nearby mountains. From there, they cast their newborn children over the edge for the Spaniards to eat, thinking that this act would

---

23. Somondoco.

appease the anger of the men whom they believed had come from the sky.[24]

But more than anything else, the Indians feared horses; so great was this fear that it is difficult even to imagine. Nevertheless, as best they possibly could, the Spaniards behaved in a most friendly manner, trying to make the Indians understand their peaceful intentions; and thus, little by little their fears began to subside. And when the Indians realized that the Christians were just men, like them, they decided to test their fortune against them, which they did when the Christians were in the province of Bogotá, deep inside the New Kingdom. There, the Indians came out to meet them in battle, marching forward with great order and discipline. However, despite their numbers, which we mentioned above, they were easily defeated. When they saw the horses galloping toward them, so great was their fright that they all turned their backs and ran. The same thing occurred in the province of Tunja. For that reason, it is not necessary to provide specific accounts of each military encounter or skirmish that the Christians have had with those barbarians. Suffice it to say that most of the year 1537 and part of 1538 was spent in subjugating them, some through peaceful methods, and others through necessary force. In the end, the two provinces of Tunja and Bogotá were left well subjugated, and the Indians firmly under the just obedience that is owed to Your Majesty.

The nation and province of the Panches was left equally subjugated, in spite of the fact that the Panches are a more indomitable and tougher people than the Moxcas. And not only are they more valiant,

24. Francisco Salguero, who testifies in Bartolomé Camacho's *probanza de mérito*, relates a similar tale. Salguero claims that when the Spaniards first arrived in Muisca territory, at the town of Guachetá, a group of natives came down from the nearby mountains to meet them. Thinking that the Spaniards were cannibals, they offered Jiménez several young children to sacrifice. See servicios y méritos de Bartolomé Camacho, AGI Patronato 157, N. 1, R. 2, fol. 116v. Earlier in the same *probanza*, Camacho makes the same claim. Ibid., fol. 81v. It should be noted, however, that neither Salguero nor Camacho suggests that the Indians offered these sacrificial victims because they considered the Spaniards gods. And while this perception is a common feature of later colonial chronicles and modern historical accounts, it is not something that the participants themselves claim. In his recent study of the Jiménez expedition, José Ignacio Avellaneda Navas accepts the view that the Muisca considered the Spaniards gods and that for this reason alone they revered the newcomers, showing them their secret shrines, the residences of their lords, the location of the emerald mines, and their gold. See Avellaneda Navas, *Expedición de Gonzalo Jiménez de Quesada*, 339. In the absence of more convincing evidence, however, such a claim should be viewed with skepticism.

but they also are aided by the difficult terrain in which they reside, which consists of densely forested and rough mountains, where it was not possible take advantage of the horses. For those reasons, the Panches believed that they would not suffer the same fate as that which had befallen their neighbors; however, they thought wrong. What happened to them was precisely the same; and one after the other, they all fell under Your Majesty's rule.

In this New Kingdom, which is made up of the provinces of Bogotá and Tunja, the people are less warlike; during battle, they issue great war cries and shouts. For weapons, they fight with certain arrows, which they throw using a kind of arm sling. Others also fight with *macanas*, which are swords made from hard palm wood; they wield them with two hands, and with them they strike fierce blows. They also fight with lances, which have sharp tips burned at one end. These lances are also made from palm, and can reach sixteen or seventeen hands in length. These Indians have a strange custom when they go to war: they take the bodies of the deceased warriors who had acquired great fame in warfare; they prepare their bodies for combat, rubbing certain sticky oils over them to ensure that their armor and their weapons do not come loose. Certain Indians then carry the dead on their backs and into battle; they do this so that everyone else would understand that they fought just as the deceased had fought in their time. And they believe that the sight of the deceased ancestors in combat shames the other Indians into carrying out their duties. Thus, when they first engaged the Spaniards in battle, many Indians marched into battle with those dead warriors on their backs.

The Panches are a more valiant people than the Moxcas. They go about completely naked, covering only their private parts, and their weapons are far more lethal. The Panches fight with bows and arrows, and they use much longer lances than those carried by the Moxcas. They also fight with slings, long shields, and *macanas* for swords. Each warrior employs all of these armaments, and each fights only in the following manner: Panche warriors carry very tall shields, which protect them from head to toe. These shields are lined with animal hides, which are hollowed on the inside; and inside that hole the Panche warriors store all the above-mentioned weapons. If they choose to fight with a lance, they pull the lance from the opening in the shield through which it is stored; and when they tire of that weapon, they remove the bow and arrows, or whatever other weapon they desire, from the very same hole in the shield. Because these shields are made from leather, they weigh little, allowing the Panche warriors to carry them on their backs; and when necessary for defense, they hold the shields out front. As opposed to the Moxcas, the Panches fight in complete silence. However, they also have a very curious custom when it comes to warfare: they send only women to make peace or to negotiate settlement terms with their enemies, thinking that nothing can be denied to these women. They consider that these women possess greater strength and fortitude with which to make their pleas and pacify their enemies.

In terms of the life, customs, religion, and other matters related to the Indians of this New Kingdom, I say that the general disposition of these people is the best ever seen in the Indies, especially the women, who have pretty faces and fine figures, and do not exhibit any of the disgraceful manners that we have seen among the women of other regions. Furthermore, neither the men nor the women are as dark skinned as people in other parts of the Indies. Both the men and the women wear *mantas* of white, black, and other colors; these *mantas* fit tightly over their bodies and cover them from chest to feet. And instead of capes or robes, they drape more *mantas* over their shoulders, and thus they all go about with their bodies entirely covered. On their heads they usually wear some type of garland, made from cotton, with different-colored roses around it; these flowers match the color of the cotton, and they are placed at the front. On occasion, some of the principal *caciques* wear hats made from the cotton they cultivate in that region, which is the only material they have to make clothing. At times, some of the wives of these *caciques* wear netted bonnets.

As previously mentioned, this territory boasts a frigid climate; however, it is such a mild cold that it is not a great bother or discomfort; nor does it take anything away from the marvelous splendor of this land when one first enters into it. And the climate remains fairly uniform all year round because, in spite of the fact that there is a distinct summer during which the soils turn dry, there is not really any notable difference in temperature between summer and winter. Because of the region's proximity to the Equinoctial line, over the entire year the length of the day is the same as that of the night. It is a remarkably healthy land, much more so than the many others hitherto encountered.

In spite of the fact that their houses and buildings are made from wood and are covered in the long thatch that is native to that region, they still reflect the most marvelous workmanship and design ever seen. This is especially true of the private residences of the *caciques* and principal men, which are like palaces, encircled by many walls. These palaces look similar to the manner in which the Labyrinth of Troy is portrayed in paintings here in Spain. The houses boast great patios, with very tall relief figurative carvings throughout; and they are also filled with paintings.

The diet of these people is the same as that in other parts of the Indies, although somewhat more varied. In addition to their principal sources of food, which are maize and yuca, they also grow two or three other kinds of crops, which greatly enhance their diet. One of these crops, which they call *yomas*, is quite similar to the potato; the others, which they call *cubíos*, are more like turnips. They add these ingredients to their stews, and they too form an important part of their daily sustenance. In the very land of Bogotá, there is an infinite quantity of salt because there are salt pools; from them they make great quantities of large salt blocks. The blocks are then traded throughout the region, especially in the Sierra de Opón, and from there, as mentioned earlier, down to the Río Grande. The meats consumed by the Indians in that region include deer meat, of which there is an infinite supply; in fact, there are so many deer that they provide as much sustenance as cattle here in Spain. They also eat another kind of animal, similar to a rabbit, which they also have in great quantities. They call these animals *fucos*, but in Santa Marta and all along the northern coast, where they also are found, they are called *curies*.[25] There are few edible birds; they do have some turtle-doves, and there are a fair number of waterfowl in the lakes. There are many fish in the kingdom's rivers and lakes; and although there is not necessarily a great abundance, they are the finest ever encountered, with a taste unlike any other. And there is only one kind of fish. It is not very large, perhaps one *palmo*[26] in length, and never more than two; regardless, it is truly a splendid thing to eat.

The moral life of these Indians and the nature of their government and public order is one of moderate reason. Crimes are justly

25. Guinea pigs.
26. A *palmo* is a measurement equivalent to about twenty-one centimeters.

punished, especially murder and theft; and as far as the nefarious sin is concerned, they are most innocent, which is quite something for being Indians. Furthermore, there are more gallows spread along the roads, with more men locked in them, than one finds anywhere in Spain. They also cut off noses and ears for lesser offenses. Punishments of public shame and disgrace are reserved for principal figures; these punishments include tearing the offender's clothing, or having his hair shorn, which for them is a great disgrace.

The reverence with which these Indians honor their *caciques* is very great indeed. Never do they look their *caciques* directly in the face, even if they are engaged in familiar conversation. And should they enter a room in which their *cacique* is present, they enter with their backs toward him, and approach him thus. Whether they are seated or standing, they always have their backs to their lords, as a sign of honor.

In terms of their marriage practices, no words are spoken, and no ceremonies are performed when they wed; instead, the man simply takes the woman with him to his house. They marry as often as they like, and with as many women as they can support. Thus, depending on his wealth and his status, one man can have ten wives, while another may have as many as twenty. And Bogotá, who was king of all the *caciques*, had more than four hundred. Marriage in the first degree that is, a union between parents and children, or brothers and sisters, is expressly forbidden; and in some parts of the New Kingdom marriage in the second degree is also prohibited.

Sons do not inherit either their fathers' property or their offices; rather, everything is passed to the deceased man's brothers. And if there are no living brothers, the entire inheritance goes to the deceased brother's sons. However, their sons do not inherit from their fathers either; instead, the inheritance then passes to the father's nephews or cousins. Otherwise, they follow the same customs that we do here in Spain, except that these barbarians honor this indirect line of succession.

These Indians divide time into months and years, and do so with very specific intent. During the first ten days of each month they consume a certain herb, which the Indians along the northern coast call *hayo*.[27] They devote the following ten days to their crops and to domestic tasks. The final ten days that remain in each month are

27. Coca leaf.

spent inside their houses, where they converse with their wives and take their pleasure with them. Men and women do not share the same room, but rather the women all share one room while the man sleeps in the other. The manner in which the months are divided is done differently in some parts of the New Kingdom, where the Indians increase the time and the number of days they dedicate to each one [of the above-mentioned activities].

Those who are to become *caciques* or captains, whether they are male or female, are taken as very young children and confined within certain houses. There they remain for a number of years, depending on the nature and quality of the position they hope to inherit. There are men who have spent as many as seven years living in such isolation. And the conditions of their confinement are so strict that over the entire period they are never permitted to set their eyes on the sun; should they do so, they would relinquish the office to which they aspire. They have servants there with them, who provide them with certain specific and special meals. No one else is permitted to enter those houses. Every once in a while these same servants enter those houses and administer a great number of terrible lashings; and the Indians confined to those houses endure this penitence over the course of the entire period I mentioned above. However, once they leave this confinement, they are permitted to pierce their ears and their noses with gold rings, which among these Indians is a symbol of great honor. They also wear gold plates, which cover their chests, and gold hats, similar to miters, as well as gold armlets. These people are mad about their songs and their dances, and these are their pleasures. These people are also great liars, as are all the people of the Indies. They just never learn how to tell the truth. They are a people of moderate talent when it comes to crafting things such as gold jewelry and copying what they see in our own jewels; the same might be said of their efforts to imitate our way of making cloth from their cotton. However, as jewel makers they are not as capable as New Spain's Indians; and in terms of making cloth they are not as skillful as the Indians from Peru.

In terms of the religion of these Indians, I say that in their false and mistaken ways, they are deeply religious. In addition to each town having its own temples, which the Spaniards there call sanctuaries, they also have a great many temples outside their towns; and they have built numerous roads and paths that extend from their towns and lead directly to those very temples. Furthermore, they have an infinite number of hermitages in the mountains, along the roads, and in different parts of the kingdom. And all of these houses of worship contain great quantities of gold and emeralds. They perform sacrifices in these temples, with blood, water and fire, which they do in the following manner: they kill large numbers of birds, and scatter the blood around the temple; then they decapitate the birds and leave their heads hanging within the same temples. They do not perform sacrifices with human blood, unless it is in one of two manners. The first is if they happen to capture some young boy in warfare against their enemies, the Panches. Their goal is to seize a boy who looks young enough not to have engaged in sexual relations with a woman; once back in their territory, they sacrifice the boy inside their sanctuary, with the ritual murder accompanied by loud cries and shouts. The other method of sacrifice involves the young male priests they have for their temples; each *cacique* has one, but few have two because they are extremely expensive. And the Indians purchase the boys in a province called La Casa del Sol the House of the Sun, where these *mojas* are raised.[28] The Casa del Sol is located roughly thirty leagues distance from the New Kingdom.[29] As mentioned above, these boys are then brought to the New Kingdom to serve in the sanctuaries. And they are venerated so highly that they are always carried around on shoulders. They are killed when they reach an age when they appear old enough to have sexual relations with women. The killing takes place inside the temples, and the blood is offered to their idols. However, should a *moja* happen to have physical contact with a woman before the ritual takes place, he is then spared from sacrifice because it is said that his blood is not sufficiently potent to placate sins.

28. The sixteenth-century Spanish chronicler Gonzalo Fernández de Oviedo y Valdés described these *mojas* as young boys, age five or six years old. According to Oviedo, the Muisca acquired these *mojas* from a distant province where it was said that they spoke to the sun. See Gonzalo Fernández de Oviedo y Valdés, *Historia general y natural de las Indias*, 5 vols., ed. Juan Pérez de Tudela Bueso (Madrid: Atlas, 1959), vol. 2, book 26, chapter 28, p. 402.

29. According to the sixteenth-century chronicler Friar Pedro Aguado, the Casa del Sol was located just north of Muisca territory, in a province inhabited by an indigenous group he called Laches. Aguado claimed that this "House of the Sun" boasted a great abundance of gold, that large numbers of Muiscas were buried there, and that others made pilgrimages to the house to practice idolatry. See Aguado, *Recopilación historial*, 1.3:317.

Before one lord engages in warfare against another, all the people from both sides gather in front of their temples. They sing all day and all night, pausing only for the few hours when they withdraw to have a meal or to sleep. In those songs they plead with the sun, the moon, and to the other idols they worship, asking them to grant them victory. In these songs they relate all the just causes they have for waging that war. Should they emerge victorious, over many days they offer their thanks to their idols in precisely the same way. If they are routed, they sing a great lamentation for their defeat. In their false religion, they have many consecrated forests and lakes, where they would not dare to cut a tree or take a drop of water for anything in the world. They go into these forests to perform their sacrifices, and they bury gold and emeralds in them. And they are most certain that no person would touch their offerings because they all believe that anyone who tampers with such offerings would then fall dead. The same can be said of the lakes that they have dedicated for their sacrifices: they go and toss in great quantities of gold and precious stones, which remain lost forever. These Indians consider the sun and the moon as the creators of all things, and they believe that the two united as husband and wife, and that they engage in sexual relations. In addition to that belief, they also possess a great number of idols, which they worship in the same way that we worship our saints here [in Spain]. They pray to these idols, asking them intercede on their behalf before the sun and the moon. And thus, each one of their sanctuaries or temples is dedicated to the name of one of these idols. In addition to the idols in the temples, every Indian, no matter how poor, has his own idol, or two, or three, or more. These idols are exactly the same as the ones possessed by the gentiles in their time, which were called *lares*. These household idols are made from very fine gold; and in a hole in the idol's belly they place many emeralds, in accordance with the wealth of the idol's owner. If the Indian is too poor to have a gold idol in his house, he has one made out of wood; he also places as much gold and as many emeralds as he is able into the hole in the idol's belly.[30] These domestic idols are small in size;

30.   Further examples of such practices in Muisca territory can be found in J. Michael Francis, "'In the service of God, I order that these temples of idolatrous worship be razed to the ground': Extirpation of Idolatry and the Search for the *Santuario Grande* of Iguaque," in *Colonial Lives: Documents on Latin American History, 1550–1850*, ed. Richard Boyer and Geoffrey Spurling (Oxford: Oxford University Press, 2000), 39–53.

the largest ones are roughly the same length as the distance between the hand and the elbow. And their devotion to these idols is so strong that they do not go anywhere, whether it is to work their fields, or to any other place, at any time, without them. They carry their idols in a small basket, which hangs from their arms. And what is most alarming is that they even carry them to war as well; with one arm they fight, and with the other they hold their idol. This is especially true in the province of Tunja, where the Indians are deeply religious.

In terms of burial practices, the Indians inter the dead in two different ways. They bind the corpses tightly in cloth, having first removed the intestines and the rest of their insides. Then they fill the empty stomachs with gold and emeralds. They also place much gold around the corpse and on top of it, before tightly wrapping the entire corpse in cloth. They build a type of large bed, which sits just above the ground inside certain sanctuaries, which are used only for that purpose, and are dedicated to the deceased. They then place the corpses there and leave them on top of those beds, without ever burying them; this practice later proved to be of no small benefit to the Spaniards.

The other method they use to inter the dead is in water, in the great lakes. The deceased is placed inside a coffin; they may add gold, depending on the status of the deceased. Then they add as much gold and emeralds as they can fit inside the coffin. With all the gold and the emeralds inside the coffin, together with the body of the deceased, they drop the coffin into the deepest depths of the deepest lakes.

As far as the immortality of the soul is concerned, they hold such barbarous and confused beliefs about the matter that it is impossible to accept what they say; namely, they place the ultimate rest and peace of the dead in both the body and the soul as one. They believe that those who lead good lives, and not bad ones, are rewarded with a great rest, with many pleasures; those who lead bad lives endure terrible hardships, and receive a great many lashes. Those who were dedicated to providing sustenance to the population also join the good when they die, where they enjoy much rest and many pleasures; and they do so for that reason alone, even if they had led bad lives. They also believe that those who die in battle, as well as the women who die in childbirth, go directly to a place of rest and pleasure. And they do so for one reason alone: the willingness with which they both worked to help the republic expand and grow. And it matters not that before their deaths they had led wicked and contemptible lives.

In the land and nation of the Panche, which surrounds this New Kingdom, there is very little about their religion and moral life that is worth relating because they are such a bestial people that they do not worship or believe in anything but their own wicked acts and vices. Nor do they respect any rules or norms whatsoever. The Panches are a people who refuse to exchange their gold, or anything else for that matter, unless it is for something they can eat and from which they can take pleasure; they are especially willing to trade if it allows them to acquire human flesh to eat, which is their greatest vice. And it is for that purpose that they always launch attacks and wage war in the New Kingdom. For the most part, Panche territory is rich in food and provisions. However, there is a section that has less abundance, and yet another that is even less fertile. In fact, the conditions are absolutely miserable in one part of Panche territory, which borders the province of Tunja, between two large rivers and several mountains. There, as the Spaniards carried out the conquest of the area, they came across a province of people, not small in population, whose only source of food was ants. They mash those ants into a type of bread, which they eat.[31] There is a great abundance of those ants, and the Indians in that very province raise them for food, keeping them in enclosed pens made from tall leaves. And in that province there is a great diversity of ants, some large in size and others small.

---

31. Andrés Vázquez de Molina, a veteran of the Jiménez *jornada*, testified that he and the other Spaniards suffered from such hunger over the course of the expedition that they ate ants, as well as the bread that the Indians make from them. See servicios y méritos de Nicolás Gutierrez, AGI Patronato 165, N. 3, R. 2, fol. 803r.

Pirú! Pirú! Pirú! Good Licenciado Jiménez, I dare say that this

is another Cajamarca.

5

Treasure, Torture, and the *Licenciado*'s Return

The two-year period between August 1537 and July 1539 witnessed some of the most dramatic and tragic events of the Spanish conquest of New Granada.[1] Jiménez and his men sacked the Muisca shrines at Tunja and Sogamoso, and they launched a surprise attack on Bogotá's mountain retreat, which resulted in the *cacique*'s controversial death. They launched expeditions to explore the vast plains (*llanos*) that extended both east and west from Muisca territory, and they followed rumors of distant tribes of Amazon women.

Over the same period, Jiménez formalized a military alliance with Bogotá's successor, Sagipa, and joined the new *cacique* in a campaign against his bitter enemies, the Panches. But this alliance came at a price. On their return from the Panche campaign, Jiménez demanded that Sagipa surrender all of his predecessor's treasure. Sagipa was placed under house arrest and subjected to torture. At one point his body was bound tightly, his feet put to the torch, and boiling animal fat poured over his naked chest.[2] Within days, Sagipa died from his wounds.

Soon after Sagipa's death, Jiménez's small force received unexpected visitors. In February 1539 Nicolás Federmán's expedition had arrived from the governorship of Venezuela; less than two months later, another expeditionary force, this one led by Sebastián de Belalcázar, had arrived from Quito (see Map 3).[3] It was with Belalcázar's arrival in

---

1. According to the sixteenth-century chronicler Juan de Castellanos, the Spanish capture of the *cacique* of Tunja, with all of his gold and emeralds, led Jiménez's men to shout with great joy that they had found another Cajamarca, hence the epigraph to this chapter. However, I have found no other reference to such a claim in any of the extensive *probanzas de méritos* or in any other firsthand account of the conquest of Tunja. See Castellanos, *Elegías de varones ilustres de Indias*, 1200.

2. For detailed testimonies of Sagipa's arrest and subsequent torture, see AGI Escribanía 1006A, fols. 26r–49v. In early February 1547, Gonzalo Jiménez de Quesada was charged and found guilty of Sagipa's torture and death. Jiménez was fined 100 *ducados*, his title of captain was suspended for six years, and he was forbidden to return to Santa Marta and the New Kingdom of Granada for one year. Ibid., 49r–49v.

3. Avellaneda Navas, *Conquerors of the New Kingdom of Granada*, 36–39.

Muisca territory that Jiménez finally learned of don Pedro Fernández de Lugo's death. At Belalcázar's urging, Jiménez decided to establish three new cities in the region, an act that he believed would help his claims to the new territory. Thus, on April 27, 1539, Jiménez founded the city of Santa Fe de Bogotá, future capital of the New Kingdom of Granada; months later the cities of Vélez and Tunja were also founded.[4]

We resume the story in August 1537, almost six months after Jiménez and his men arrived in Muisca territory. Pedro Fernández de Valenzuela had just returned from the emerald mines near Somondoco, discussed in the previous chapter. Jiménez had heard rumors of a nearby settlement called Tunja, whose *cacique* was said to possess great quantities of gold and emeralds. On hearing these reports, Jiménez quickly gathered a small force and rushed toward Tunja.

The sacking of Tunja yielded the single greatest haul of treasure in the entire conquest of Muisca territory; it was, as the epigraph to this chapter suggests, New Granada's Cajamarca, although on a much smaller scale. The registered spoils from the sacking of Tunja represented almost 72 percent of all the *oro fino* collected between May 1536 and May 1538. The fourteen thousand pesos of *oro bajo* gathered in Tunja was roughly 37 percent of all the low-grade ore collected over the same period; and the 280 emeralds recorded that Monday represented the single largest "official" entry for the precious stones, and 17 percent of the total number of emeralds recorded in the logbook.

After setting aside the royal fifth, Jiménez and his captains agreed that before they divided the remaining spoils, they needed to award compensation for certain goods and services, as well as for lost horses. They also decided to grant merit pay to individuals whose acts of bravery helped ensure the expedition's success. Only then would the remaining gold and emeralds be divided into shares and the shares be distributed among the survivors.[5]

Between March 1537, when Jiménez and his men first entered Muisca territory, and June 1538, when they agreed to distribute the booty, only six Spaniards had lost their lives. Thus 173 men were

4. Ibid., 39.

5. After setting aside the Crown's royal fifth, another 2,500 pesos were removed from the total spoils as compensation to the nineteen men who lost horses during the expedition. Another 7,315 pesos were awarded as compensation for a wide range of goods and services, and a total of 3,885 pesos were distributed in merit pay. Only then was the remaining booty divided into shares. For details of the distribution of all the gold and emeralds, see AGI Escribanía 1006A, Cuaderno 5, fols. 9v–17r.

entitled to receive some part of the total treasure.[6] Each share was valued at 510 pesos of *oro fino*, fifty-seven pesos of *oro bajo*, and five emeralds. Of course, it is highly unlikely that all the gold and the emeralds found their way into the official logbook. Emeralds especially would have been easy to conceal and therefore it is reasonable to assume some level of fraud.

However, in a venture that involved dividing spoils among almost two hundred men, excessive fraud was probably mitigated by the potential consequences. For example, in July 1538 Jiménez learned that one of the horsemen, Juan Tafur, had attempted to conceal sixty-five pesos of *oro fino* and 122 pesos of *oro bajo* from the rest of the company; Jiménez's response was to order Tafur's execution. Earlier, Jiménez had sentenced another Spaniard to death for stealing some *mantas* from local natives.[7] And while Tafur's life ultimately was spared, those who attempted to hoard large quantities of treasure from the rest of the company did so at the risk of being denounced by a disgruntled colleague.

Therefore, apart from the few stones and gold objects safely kept hidden from others, nearly half the men on the expedition (eighty-six out of 180) received one share of the total booty; the two priests and all the horsemen (forty-two men in all) were entitled to two shares. Twelve men, including Jiménez's brother Hernán Pérez de Quesada, as well as all the captains, earned four shares. The greatest number of shares, ten, were to go to Santa Marta's governor, don Pedro Fernández de Lugo,[8] with Gonzalo Jiménez de Quesada earning nine shares, worth a total of 4,590 pesos of *oro fino*, 513 pesos of *oro bajo*, and forty-five emeralds. And while this represented a handsome bounty, it is worth noting that Jiménez's nine shares barely surpassed the equivalent of one share in the conquest of Peru.[9] (See Table 5.1 for comparison)

6. See Avellaneda Navas, *Conquerors of the New Kingdom of Granada*, 36.
7. Jiménez ordered that the guilty individual, named Juan Gordo, be garroted for the theft, and in spite of the many pleas for clemency, the sentence was executed. See ibid., 36.
8. As mentioned earlier, when the shares were divided, Jiménez was unaware that Lugo had passed away. Thus don Pedro's shares were passed to his son, don Alonso Luis de Lugo.
9. Of course, Jiménez and his men gathered more booty after the official distribution of individual shares and before Jiménez returned to Spain in 1539. Official accounts suggest that between August 1538 and May 1539 the Spaniards collected another 4,204 pesos of *oro fino*, 8,475 pesos of *oro bajo*, 8,500 pesos of *chafalonía*, and 630 emeralds, most of which were obtained from the *cacique* of Bogotá. See Tovar Pinzón, *Relaciones y visitas a los Andes*, 3:39.

Table 5.1 Total Booty and Value per Share

	Total Booty Collected	Value of One Share	
Peru	1,159,865 pesos	Gold pesos	4,440
		Silver marks	181
New Granada	191,294 pesos in *oro fino*	*Oro fino*	510
	18,390 pesos in *chafalonía*		
	37,288 pesos in *oro bajo*	*Oro bajo*	57
	1,815 emeralds	Emeralds	5

Excerpt from the "Relación del Nuevo Reino: Letter from Captain Juan de San Martín and Captain Antonio de Lebrija" (July 8, 1539), AGI Patronato 27, R. 14, fols. 3v–6v

The final pages of Captain Juan de San Martín and Captain Antonio de Lebrija's letter to King Charles V relate events that unfolded between late August 1537 and July 8, 1539, the eve of their return to Spain. The letter presents an overview of the many highlights of that two-year period—the sacking of Tunja, the death of Bogotá, the expedition to the *llanos,* the campaigns against the Panches, and the search for the Amazon women. It also details the events surrounding the arrest, torture, and death of Bogotá's successor, Sagipa. As royal officials assigned to keep detailed records of the expedition's spoils, it is hardly surprising that San Martín and Lebrija provide very specific details of all the booty collected, the shares distributed, and the taxes owed to the Crown.

By this point, the more we explored the region, the more our interpreters came to understand our intentions; and they told Jiménez of a great lord named Tunja who lived very close to where we were camped. Lieutenant Jiménez thus gathered all the foot soldiers and horsemen he could and moved against Tunja. At first, on the day we entered his territory, Tunja came out to greet us, offering us signs of peace; later, having entered the town where he resided, Tunja unveiled his deception; he and his Indian subjects chose to do something other than honor the peace they had promised. For that reason, Tunja was taken captive, along with a small amount of gold and stones (emeralds); he had hidden the bulk, and the finest, of his treasure. What little there was, we gathered from the residence where he slept, and from several places of worship located next to it. The booty totaled no more than 140,000 pesos in fine gold, 30,000 in low-grade ore, and a few precious stones because, as we mentioned already, most of his treasure he had hidden.[10]

This Tunja is a powerful lord; many other lords are his subjects, and he possesses great wealth. When the *principales* of this land die, they are not buried below ground, but rather above, and some gold and emeralds are placed on their corpses. Tunja is lord over many people, but he is not as tyrannical as Bogotá.

With the men camped in Tunja, news arrived of two other *caciques*, one named Duitama and the other Sogamoso, located two and three days' march from Tunja. Jiménez went there with certain foot soldiers and horsemen, but found the towns abandoned. In Sogamoso, they found up to 40,000 pesos of fine gold, some low-grade gold, and emeralds adorning several temples of worship.[11] However, they found no Indians because they all had fled out of town. On his return to camp, Jiménez passed through the territory of the other lord, whose name was Duitama. The Indians came out to meet us, shouting, armed, and ready to bring us harm if they could. Some Indians were killed, although few, owing to the difficult terrain of the battlefield.

Having returned to Tunja, Jiménez weighed all the gold that had been collected, both in Tunja and in Sogamoso, as well other bits of gold collected here and there. It amounted to 191,294 pesos of fine gold, 37,288 pesos of low-grade gold, and 18,390 pesos of *chafalonía*.[12] There were also 1,815 emerald stones of many sizes, some large and others small, of many different qualities.

Seeing the grandeur and the incredible riches of the land in which we found ourselves, Jiménez and the captains decided to return to

10. The figures cited here vary only slightly from the ones recorded in the expedition's official logbook. The logbook entry from Monday, August 20, 1537, states that "136,000 pesos of fine gold were found in the Valley of Tunja when we captured the *cacique* of that valley; in addition, we found 14,000 pesos of low-grade gold; furthermore, there were 280 emerald stones." Despite the fact that Captain Lebrija and Captain San Martín suggest in their letter that they picked up only a few stones, the 280 emeralds recorded in the "official" list of spoils represent the single largest entry for emeralds during the entire expedition. See AGI Escribanía 1006A, Cuaderno 5, fol. 7r.

11. The official logbook entry from Tuesday, September 4, 1537, records the spoils obtained in the Valley of Sogamoso as 40,000 pesos of fine gold, 12,000 pesos of low-grade gold, and 118 emeralds. Ibid.

12. None of the Spanish accounts clarifies the nature of the items classified as *chafalonía*. The category probably refers to a wide range of gold objects for which the Spaniards had no particular use.

Bogotá. It was believed, and we had heard certain rumors, that Bogotá possessed countless riches in gold and precious stones because he was a far more powerful lord than Tunja.[13] And leaving the camp in the valley of Tunja, Jiménez gathered some foot soldiers and horsemen and moved against Bogotá, whom we found prepared for war. And the Indians did not cease to engage us in battle; the revolts and skirmishes continued day and night, putting us and our horses in great difficulty from sheer exhaustion. Several Indians taken captive during the uprising informed Jiménez that Bogotá was hiding in one of the "houses of pleasure" [casas de placer] he possessed, which was located three leagues from the valley. One night Jiménez decided to attempt to capture Bogotá, and if possible, to make friends with him. Shortly before daybreak, we moved against the cacique, skirmishing briefly with some of the Indians there. Later it was said that Bogotá was among the dead, and that he was killed without being recognized; they even say that he was disguised in the most ragged and shabby clothing. However, at the time we did not learn of his death because he died somewhere up in a mountain, without our knowledge, and with none of us as witness.[14]

Seeing the general state of war, Jiménez decided to return to the camp and renew efforts to discover the llanos and learn their secrets. In order to do that, he sent Captain Juan de San Martín, along

13. It was suggested that Bogotá's treasure exceeded ten thousand marks (more than three thousand kilograms) of gold and ten thousand emeralds. See Jorge Augusto Gamboa M., "Los caciques muiscas y la transición al regimen colonial en el altiplano cundiboyacense durante el siglo XVI (1537–1560)," in Muiscas: Representaciones, cartografías, y etnopolíticas de la memoria, ed. Ana María Gómez Londoño (Bogotá: Editorial Pontificia Universidad Javeriana, 2005), 58.

14. The precise circumstances of Bogotá's death remain something of a mystery. The few firsthand accounts of the assault on Bogotá's mountain retreat (which most other references refer to as the casa del monte and not casa de placer) are vague and often contradictory. For example, consider the 1545 "Relación de Santa Marta" (translated in Chapter 5 of this work), which blames Bogotá's death on two Spanish horsemen and two foot soldiers who murdered the cacique as he attempted to escape. The author of the Relación claims that the four Spaniards did not know the Indian's true identity and that they killed him in order to steal the rich clothing he wore. Other firsthand accounts fail to clarify the matter. Captain Juan de Céspedes testified that Bogotá had escaped through a trapdoor before being caught and killed by two Spanish horsemen who, in Céspedes's words, "not knowing what they were doing, [stabbed him] with a lance, after which he died." See servicios y méritos de Juan Ramírez de Hinojoso, AGI Patronato 158, N. 3, R. 1, fols. 396v–397r. Another veteran of the expedition, Diego de Frias, claimed that a Spanish crossbowman shot and killed Bogotá with a crossbow bolt, again unaware of his victim's true identity. See AGI Escribanía 1006A, Cuaderno 3, fol. 127r.

with certain foot soldiers and horsemen, on the discovery, advising
them that the best route [to the *llanos*] would be through Duitama.
Jiménez therefore decided to go as far as Duitama, and from there
dispatch the others on the expedition. And that was what they did;
however, they were unable to discover [the *llanos*] from that direction either, because ahead they came across a great many high, snow-
capped mountains that impeded their access.

Seeing the difficult obstacles in reaching the plains from Duitama,
Jiménez made up his mind to take some of his interpreters and
venture off to discover an alternative route to the *llanos*. Leaving the
camp behind in Tunja, with orders that they make their way to the
land of Bogotá, Jiménez departed, following a different path from
the one taken during the initial discovery, and returning to the land
of Bogotá. He arrived in the territory of a *cacique* named Pasca, who
was a subject of Bogotá. There, he heard rumors of a very rich land
called Neiva, eight days' march through uninhabited lands, where
the Indians mined gold from below the ground. And the Indians
from Pasca carry salt and other merchandise to Neiva, which they
exchange for gold; they claim that the vast plains, or *llanos*, extend
out from there. With that news, Jiménez followed the path toward
Neiva, enduring a great many hardships from the extreme cold and
icy conditions of that desolate land. On arrival, they saw that it was
indeed a land of open plains, although it did not appear to be the
same as the one with the mines. Instead, it was a valley of the same
Río Grande that extends towards Santa Marta. However, as the valley is very wide in some places, it appears to be an open plain. This
land of Neiva is different from that of Bogotá; it is extremely torrid,
sickly, and not well populated. There is fine gold as well as evidence
of silver, and there are gold mines in this land, which the natives
claim are very rich. Nevertheless, the Río Grande around Neiva was
still flooded; for that reason, and owing to the fact that many of the
people on the expedition had fallen ill, Jiménez decided to return to
the Valley of Bogotá without exploring the *llanos* any further.

From there, Jiménez sent orders to summon the rest of the camp,
which was located near the Valley of Bogotá, in the lands of a *cacique* named Suesca. Earlier, Suesca had made peace with Jiménez's
brother,[15] who had remained behind in the camp; and many other

15. Hernán Pérez de Quesada.

neighboring lords came forward with that same *cacique* to make peace. On their arrival in the Valley of Bogotá, the entire camp learned of the death of Bogotá, whom we had killed in the attack on his "house of pleasure." We also learned that Bogotá's nephew and heir, named Sagipa, had fled into the mountains around the valley, with all the deceased Bogotá's gold and precious stones. And seeing this act of rebellion, Jiménez ordered that it be proclaimed to all the neighboring *caciques* subject to Bogotá, that they come forward at once and make friends with the Spaniards. If they did not, then Jiménez would kill them and wage war against them and all of their descendants. On hearing this, in no time at all, every *cacique* came forward, with the exception of the few *caciques* who had fled with Sagipa into the mountains. Among the *caciques* who came forward was Bogotá's nephew, who is called Chía, and the lieutenant paid him much honor. Chía himself explained that the inheritance and the dominion of the deceased Bogotá belonged to him because he was the rightful heir. This Chía is a lord himself, and no one can become Bogotá without first serving as *cacique* of Chía; it is an ancient custom among them that when Bogotá dies, Chía becomes the next Bogotá, and another is chosen to be Chía. And while he serves as Chía, he does not hold dominion over any *caciques,* other than over the inhabitants of his own pueblo, where he resides.

While camped in this Valley of Bogotá, we received reports of a nation of women who live alone, without the presence of any Indian men. For that reason, we called them Amazons, and it is said that they purchase certain slaves from whom they become pregnant. And should they give birth to a boy, they send the infant to live with his father; if it is a girl, they raise her themselves. It is said that have no other use for their slaves other than for procreation; and once they become pregnant, they have the slaves returned. On hearing the strange and novel reports about that land, Jiménez sent his brother, along with some foot soldiers and horsemen, to see if what the Indians had told them were true. But owing to the mountains that blocked their path, they were unable to reach those lands.[16] However,

---

16. The primary sources are relatively quiet about the 1538 expedition, led by Jiménez's brother Hernán Pérez, to locate the Amazons, but witnesses in three sixteenth-century *probanzas de méritos* made references to it. Question 9 of Pedro Sotelo's *probanza* asked witnesses to comment on his participation in the expedition to search for the "Provinces of the Amazons." And while none of Sotelo's witnesses offered specific details about the expedition, none of them denied that it occurred or that Sotelo

they did manage to get within three or four days' walk, always hearing more rumors about those lands, and how they were extremely rich in gold.[17] It was said that the same gold that is found in this region and in Tunja comes from those lands. Along this route they discovered many valleys, with dense settlements, and very rich.

Having returned from this expedition, we [as well as Jiménez,] decided that it would be right and good that Your Majesty learn of all the services that had been performed and continue to be done in this land on your behalf. Therefore, Jiménez, in the company of several others, is now on his way to the kingdoms of Spain to kiss Your Majesty's royal hands and provide Your Majesty with a full account of everything that hitherto has occurred here. For that reason, Jiménez ordered that we distribute the shares of all the gold and precious stones that had been acquired in this land. By that point, the total booty amounted to 191,294 pesos of fine gold, 37,288 pesos of low-grade gold, 18,390 pesos of low-grade gold objects [*chafalonía*], and 1,815 emeralds of various sizes and qualities.[18] From all of this, Your Majesty was paid the royal fifth;[19] what remained was divided into shares among the [conquistadors], with each share valued at

---

participated in it. See servicios y méritos de Pedro de Sotelo, AGI Patronato 156, R. 11, fols. 1128v–1178v. Nicolás Gutiérrez's 1583 *probanza* also made passing reference to the discovery of the Amazons. See servicios y méritos de Nicolás Gutiérrez, AGI Patronato 165, N. 3, R. 2, fol. 779v. Perhaps the most revealing testimonies about the Amazons came from Diego Romero's 1561 *probanza*, in which Captain Juan de Céspedes and Juan de Montalvo both offered details about the expedition. The two witnesses discussed the capture of a local *cacica* (female chief) named Furatena, who governed the said province. Montalvo claimed that the natives from that province were called Amazons because they fought with arrows, but he added that they were not in fact real Amazons, a belief shared by Diego Romero. Romero testified that the Amazons were not discovered on the expedition because they did not exist. See servicios y méritos de Diego Romero, AGI Patronato, 154, N. 3, R. 1, fols. 504v–505r, 524r–524v, and 535r–535v.

17. Hernán Pérez de Quesada did not return from the expedition empty-handed. On Sunday, May 12, 1538, the expedition's official logbook records that on his return from the "Provincia de las Amazonas," Pérez added 2,850 pesos in fine gold, 3,600 pesos in low-grade ore, and ninety-four emeralds, to the expedition's coffers. See AGI Escribanía 1006A, Cuaderno 5, fols. 7v–8r.

18. These are the same figures that were recorded in the expedition's logbook on June 13, 1538. This is hardly surprising considering that Antonio de Lebrija served as the expedition's treasurer; he was responsible for ensuring that all the treasure was accurately recorded and that the king received his royal fifth. Nevertheless, as we will see below, there is a discrepancy between the royal fifth recorded in the logbook and the totals cited by Captain San Martín and Captain Lebrija. See ibid., fol. 13r.

19. According to the official logbook from the expedition, the Crown's royal fifth should have totaled 38,259 pesos of fine gold, 7,257 pesos of low-grade ore, 3,690 pesos of *chafalonía*, and 363 emeralds. Ibid., fols. 13r–13v. However, Captain San Martín and

510 pesos of fine gold, 57 pesos of low-grade gold, and five emerald stones.[20]

With the lieutenant's plans to leave for Spain already made public, Bogotá (Sagipa) decided to come meet with Jiménez, having witnessed the excellent care with which the lieutenant had treated all the *caciques* who had made peace with the Spaniards. Sagipa also had realized the misery of life as a rebel, away from his home, and with so many of his Indian followers either captured or killed. Jiménez received him with every honor and good treatment he possibly could, and Sagipa agreed to remain under Your Majesty's obedience. Seeing the respect with which he had been treated, Sagipa begged Jiménez to provide him with some Spanish soldiers that he could take with him in battle against his nearby enemies, the Panches. In order to please Sagipa and also to confirm that we were indeed loyal allies to our friends, Jiménez acquiesced.[21] And upon his return from Panche territory, Jiménez reminded Sagipa that as our friend, he must also perform the good deeds of a friend. Sagipa already knew how his uncle, the previous Bogotá, was our enemy, and he was still our enemy when we killed him. Therefore, all the gold and the precious stones that the previous Bogotá possessed belong to Your Majesty and to Your Majesty's Spanish subjects, and Sagipa should have them

---

Captain Lebrija cite rather different figures, in spite of the fact that they record the same total of treasure found in the official logbook. Their letter claims that the royal fifth amounted to 29,100 pesos of fine gold, 8,800 pesos of low-grade gold, 5,600 pesos of *chafalonía*, and 562 emeralds.

20. In order to avoid conflicts over the distribution of the emeralds, the three men elected by their peers to oversee the fair division of spoils (Captain Juan de San Martín, Baltasar Maldonado, and Juan Valenciano) decided to separate all the stones into five different piles; as each soldier arrived to collect his share, Jiménez would remove one emerald from each of the five piles. Ibid., fol. 18r. The names of each recipient and the corresponding number of shares appear in the same document, fols. 15v–17r. Of course, it is likely that individual Spaniards accumulated far more booty than the official logbook recorded. For example, when Diego de Aguilar returned to Spain in 1539, he brought with him seventy-five emeralds that had been entrusted to him by Juan Tafur. When the booty was distributed in June of 1538, Tafur received his corresponding share of ten emeralds; how and where he obtained the other sixty-five stones is unclear, but it is unlikely that Tafur was the only Spaniard to possess far more than his official share of spoils. See Avellaneda Navas, *Expedición de Gonzalo Jiménez de Quesada*, 305.

21. A number of witnesses later testified that Jiménez gathered a group of Spanish foot soldiers and horsemen and joined Sagipa on the military campaign to Panche territory. For example, see the testimony of Francisco de San Martín, AGI Escribanía 1006, Cuaderno 3, fols. 67v–68r.

brought forward and given to us because they were our enemy's possessions. Sagipa responded that he did not possess the treasure, and that his uncle had distributed it in many parts of the region; but Sagipa later confessed that he did have it.

Upon hearing how Sagipa carried on raving such nonsense, Jiménez brought the *cacique* with him to the camp, gave him a house in which to stay, and placed him under Spanish guard. And he told Sagipa to hand over all his uncle's gold and emeralds; until then, he would not be permitted to leave the house. On hearing this, Bogotá claimed that he would fill the little house next to his with gold and many precious stones, all within a period of twenty days. In the aforementioned house where he was held, Sagipa was given every possible care, and provided with Indian men and women to serve him.

The agreed twenty-day period expired, and nothing of what had been promised was delivered. Seeing this, Jiménez let Sagipa know that it was a very bad thing to mock Christians, and that he should not have done that. Sagipa responded that he would still have the gold and emeralds brought, and that his subjects were in the process of collecting the treasure; but it all seemed to be nothing more than a great lie, and that his true intention was to bring us nothing more than false promises. Therefore, before he continued on his journey to Spain to report to Your Majesty, Jiménez decided to have Sagipa placed in shackles. The lieutenant then departed, leaving in his place his brother, Hernán Pérez. Jiménez continued on his journey until he reached a town they call Tinjacá; from there, he decided to go in person to see the emerald mines, about which Your Majesty will be informed by Jiménez himself, as well as from others who desire to serve Your Majesty.

Jiménez then made his way back from the mines in order to join the others and continue the journey toward the town of La Tora, where they planned to construct the brigs to sail downriver to Santa Marta. While we were in this land, which is the land of the above-mentioned Amazon women, we heard some very curious rumors that the amount of gold that these women possess is incalculable. We also heard tales of a province called Menza, located on the slopes of the *llanos*, impossible to reach; the Indians claim that the people of that province are all very rich, and that they have a house which is dedicated to the sun, and in which they perform certain sacrifices and ceremonies. And in that house they have an infinite quantity of gold and precious stones. It is said that the inhabitants of that province live in stone dwellings, that they wear clothes and shoes, and they fight with lances and clubs.

We were also told that the Bogotá, who was being held prisoner, also possessed a house filled with great quantities of gold and precious stones. Upon hearing such fantastic and novel news, it appeared to Jiménez and everyone else with him, that it would be a much better service to Your Majesty to investigate these places and bring Your Majesty a much more reliable account, even if that meant postponing our return for another year. We therefore went back to the Valley of Bogotá where the rest of the camp had remained.

On our return to the valley, Jiménez began proceedings against the imprisoned Bogotá, gathering testimony from many of the lords in this land. The investigations revealed that Sagipa possessed more than just one *bohío* filled with gold and a great many emerald stones. The *cacique* was ordered to turn over the riches, in exchange for certain rewards and recompense. He promised he would hand it over, but he never did. Instead, Sagipa's subjects, seeing their leader imprisoned and somewhat battered, escaped with the treasure. Owing to the fact that Sagipa was a noble Indian of frail stature, he passed away in prison, having been subjected to very few hardships. And thus, for the moment, Bogotá's riches have not been found because all of the Indian leaders loyal to Sagipa, and their subjects, took the gold and fled into the mountains, where they have gathered strength. And the natives of this land even say that they have chosen another Bogotá already, whom they obey and consider their lord.

A few days later Jiménez journeyed to the land of the Panches, at the request of an ally Indian *cacique* who wished to seek revenge on the Panches for some damage they had inflicted on him. During that expedition, we came across the great river that we had seen earlier at Neiva, and it was the same that flows down to Santa Marta. It is located roughly twenty leagues from the city of Santa Fe; this discovery is remarkably fortuitous for the well-being of this land, owing to the fact that brigs can be built in that place, thus making Santa Marta reachable within ten or twelve days. Furthermore, whatever supplies are needed in this land can be brought up from that location. On this same expedition, we spotted some high, snow-capped mountains, about four or five leagues across the other bank the river, extending in both directions. Asked what peoples lived in those mountains, the

Indians with us responded that the inhabitants were people just like those who lived in the valley of Bogotá; they were said to be very rich because the vessels they use, as well as their other domestic service items, were all made from gold and silver. The Indians with us insisted that this was true, and we believe them because there is much fine gold along this river. With this news, and having caused some damage to the Panches, we returned to the camp in the valley of Bogotá.

We arrived at camp, carrying with us the fresh reports of these mountains. By then, the town that the Indians were building for us already was finished, and everyone had settled in it; we called the city Santa Fe.[22] Within a few days of our return, Jiménez resolved to send his brother and a suitable number of foot soldiers and horsemen on an expedition to the snow-capped mountains, knowing that those mountains were so close to this valley. Hernán Pérez and his men departed, well armed, and with such gladness, as if they were venturing out to sea, and with such a great desire to serve Your Majesty, as is right. Six days after they left this valley, we received reports from some Indians that large numbers of Christians, on horseback and on foot, were making their way along the Río Grande below. Amazed by this strange news, Jiménez decided that his brother and the men with him should turn around and go out to discover the identity of these people. The lieutenant therefore called for his brother's immediate return;[23] Hernán Pérez and the others came back at once to Santa Fe. Once returned, having received fresh reports of the other Spaniards, Jiménez sent his brother out again, this time with twelve horsemen, and the same number of foot soldiers, ordering them to proceed down to the river to search, until they were able to catch up with the other Spaniards and discover who they were. This was no small task, owing to the difficult conditions around the river. But they learned that the people were from Peru, and that they had come up from the governorship of don Francisco Pizarro. And as captain,

22. In a royal decree signed in Madrid on July 27, 1540, King Charles I of Spain formally granted Santa Fe the title of city. See AGI Patronato 195, R. 6, fols. 18r–18v.

23. Juan Ramírez de Hinojosa, who was with Hernán Pérez at the time, claims that they were in Sogamoso when a messenger arrived with letters from Gonzalo Jiménez in which Jiménez ordered his brother's immediate return because of the unexpected arrival of the two new Spanish camps. Two days later, Hernán Pérez and his men (including Ramírez) were back in the Spanish camp. See servicios y méritos de Juan Ramírez de Hinojosa, AGI Patronato 158, N. 3, R. 1, fols. 313v–314r.

they brought Sebastián de Benalcázar, as Your Majesty will be
informed in more detail.[24]

The men returned to our town [Santa Fe], with news of the identity of the other Christians. Eight days later we received reports that
Sebastián de Benalcázar had crossed the river and was making his
way up to the Valley of Bogotá. At the very same time, we learned
that another group of Christians was coming from the direction of
the *llanos*, the same region we have been unable to reach, which is
in the direction of the rising sun. It was said that they were large in
number, and that they brought many horses with them. We were
more than a little afraid, having no idea who those people could
be. Hearing that they were so close to us, no more than six leagues
away, Jiménez sent people out to discover who they were. And we
learned that they were the people from Venezuela, who had set out
with Nicolás Federmán as their lieutenant and general.[25] It was said
that among them came some of the people from Cubagua who had
rebelled against Jerónimo Dortal. Federmán and his followers arrived,
tired and weary from their long journey through cold, wretched,
and unpopulated wastelands. Any more hardships and surely they
all would have perished. In our camp they found all the shelter, food
and clothing needed for their complete recovery, about which Your
Majesty will be informed.[26]

At this time, Nicolás Federmán was with his camp, Sebastián
de Benalcázar with his, and all of us in our pueblo in the Valley of
Bogotá; we were all within a six-league triangle, each aware of the
others' presence. What followed is something that Your Majesty,
and anyone else who hears of it, will hold in great wonder and
amazement: that people could come together from three separate

24. José Ignacio Avellaneda Navas has written about Sebastián de Belalcázar's
expedition in two separate monographs, *Conquerors of the New Kingdom of Granada*
and *La expedición de Sebastián de Belalcázar al Mar del Norte y su llegada al Nuevo
Reino de Granada* (Bogotá: Banco de la República, 1992).

25. For details of the Federmán expedition, again see the recent studies by José
Ignacio Avellaneda Navas, *Conquerors of the New Kingdom of Granada* and *Los
compañeros de Féderman, cofundadores de Santa Fe de Bogotá* (Bogotá: Tercer Mundo
Editores, 1990).

26. Francisco de Tordehumos, a veteran of the Jiménez expedition, described the
arrival in Santa Fe of Federmán and his men in the following manner: "They arrived
completely lost and destroyed, ill, and naked, wearing [nothing but] deer skins." See
servicios y méritos de Hernando Hierro Maldonado, AGI Patronato 160, N. 1, R. 9,
fol. 387v.

governorships, as are the governorships of Peru, Venezuela, and Santa Marta, in a place so far from the sea, as distant from the South Sea as it is from the North Sea. With all three camps in a triangle, messengers moving from one camp to the other, and everyone looking to do what would be best for Your Majesty, it was Our Lord's will that in His service, and in the service of of Your Majesty, that our lieutenant [Jiménez] came to an accord with Nicolás Federmán and Sebastián de Benalcázar: all the people from Venezuela and some of those from Peru were to remain in this New Kingdom of Granada and governorship of Santa Marta, with one person given judicial authority in order to maintain the peace. The three captains agreed to go together, down the Río Grande, to Spain to kiss Your Majesty's royal hands; and each one would provide Your Majesty with a full account of everything that had happened on their respective expeditions, and what services each had performed on Your behalf. Your Majesty can be assured that both Nicolás Federmán and Captain Sebastián de Benalcázar carry wonderful news of the richness of this New Kingdom. And Your Majesty can trust that these rich lands indeed exist, and that others will be found because at present this kingdom is at peace, and there are enough Spaniards and horses to send out to search and discover.

Having reached the above-mentioned agreement, Jiménez saw that this left up to 400 men and 150 horses in the region; and it seemed to him and to everyone else that it would be in Your Majesty's best interest to colonize this city [Santa Fe], as well as two other towns. One town was left settled in a valley called La Grita,[27] located a good thirty leagues from the city of Santa Fe. The other has not been founded yet, but it was decided to build it in the province of Tunja. We believe that it will be settled soon because Jiménez left orders that it be done; and once it is, there will be three towns within an area of fifty leagues, leaving enough people to explore the surrounding regions. These towns have been colonized in Your Majesty's name; and for the well and good of each, Jiménez appointed government officials whom he considered most suitable for the offices.

Moreover, for the well being of the native peoples of this land, and even for Your Majesty's own benefit, it occurred to Jiménez and to us that the Indians should be entrusted to the deserving individuals

27. The name of this town was Vélez.

who worked to carry out the conquest, pacification and discovery
of this land, in order to supply them with food, clothing, and other
necessary items for their use.[28] That was done, and some *caciques*
have been entrusted in *encomiendas* to certain Spaniards, until such
time that Your Majesty decree what best serves his interests. These
grants were also issued because it seemed to Jiménez and to us that it
was necessary for the perpetuation of this land. However, we left the
most important *caciques* of this land unassigned, until a time when
Your Majesty decrees what best meets his interests. The *caciques* not
given in *encomienda* are the *cacique* of Bogotá, the *cacique* of Tunja,
and Somyndoco, lord of the emerald stone mines. These three remain
free until Your Majesty decrees what best serves his interest in this
matter.

All of the above-mentioned is what has occurred up until today,
from the journey from Santa Marta to the conquest and pacification
of this, your New Kingdom. Of course, we left out certain details of
little significance, of which later we can give Your Majesty account.
Everything that we have seen in this land indicates that it is a
healthy place, and extremely so because in more than two years since
we first arrived, we have not lost a single man to illness. This land is
well stocked with deer, which are hunted in great number; they also
hunt without limit other animals, similar to rabbits, which they call
curís [guinea pigs]. Moreover, there is a good supply of pork meat,
which will continue into the future because the people who came
from Peru left behind more than three hundred heads, all females
and pregnant. The rivers boast many fish, and the land bears some
fruit. Furthermore, Spanish crops will grow well because of the temperate and cool climate. In some parts they harvest large quantities of
maize every eight months. In the hills and across the plains this land
is quite bare; there is little wood, except along the slopes of all the
mountains. The people wear cotton clothing, different from what is
worn in Santa Marta and in Peru. The clothing is very fine, and most
of it is painted by brush. The buildings are all made from thatch; they

28. In 1583 Miguel Ruíz Corredor, the son of Pedro Ruíz Corredor, a veteran of
the Jiménez expedition, prepared his own *probanza de mérito*. The *probanza* includes
a copy of Pedro Corredor's original *encomienda* grant from May 9, 1539. The original
grant, signed by Jiménez de Quesada, was written on deer hide because of the paucity
of paper. See servicios y méritos de Miguel Ruíz Corredor, AGI Patronato 163, R. 4,
fols. 294v–295r.

are very large, especially the houses of the lords, which are enclosed by two, sometimes three, walls. And for being made out of thatch, these dwellings are quite something to see. The lords of this land are very highly respected and regarded by their Indians, so much so that whenever they come across their leaders, they are to lower their heads as a sign of their great obedience.

These Indians are idolatrous; they sacrifice small children, as well as parrots and other birds to the sun; and they burn emerald stones. And it is said that the greater the lord, the more precious the stones that are offered to the sun. They perform other kinds of heathen rituals. Many parts of this land contain very rich mines, and the Indians are attentive and tame. They prefer peace to war because, in spite of the fact that they are many in number, they possess few offensive weapons.

The Panche Indians, who reside between the Río Grande and this land of Bogotá, are bellicose and warlike Indians. They use terrible weapons such as arrows, slings, darts, and clubs that they wield like swords. They also carry shields, and they take advantage of all of these weapons in warfare. And they eat one another, even raw, not bothering to roast or cook the flesh. And it matters not that their victims are from the same nation and towns. They go about naked because the climate is so torrid. These Panches and the Indians from Bogotá engage in fierce warfare. If the Panches capture Indians from Bogotá they either kill them or eat them later. And if the Indians from Bogotá kill or capture some Panches, they decapitate them and carry the heads back to place in their shrines. However, if they capture young children, they bring them back alive and take them high up to the mountain peaks, where they use them in certain rituals and sacrifices. For many days, they all sing together to the sun; it is said that the sun consumes the blood of those children, which it greatly desires, taking far greater pleasure from the blood of children than it does from the blood of adults.

On May 12, 1539, as we prepared to depart for Spain to report to Your Majesty, Jiménez appointed some officials who, on Your Majesty's behalf, took possession of the royal chest that we kept in this New Kingdom. The chest remains in the hands of these officials, and it contains the gold that corresponds to Your Majesty's royal fifth, a total of 29,100 pesos of fine gold, 8,800 pesos of low-grade gold, and 5,600 pesos of *chafalonía*.

Lieutenant Jiménez departs on this very day for Spain to report to Your Majesty. In addition to the gold that remains in the chest mentioned above, Jiménez carries with him eleven thousand pesos of fine gold to show Your Majesty a sample of the quality of the gold in this land. Moreover, he has all the emeralds that correspond to Your Majesty's royal fifth, which amounts to 562 stones; it is believed that among them are many of very great value.

Having occurred everything mentioned above, the lieutenant and the captains mentioned above, together with us and up to thirty more men, embarked on the Río Grande. We departed from a town called Guataquí, where we had constructed the two brigs to sail to Santa Marta. Roughly thirty leagues downriver we came across some fierce rapids, which we passed with great difficulty and risk to our lives. Twelve days later we arrived at the mouth of the river at the sea. Turning toward the city of Santa Marta, from where we had departed three years earlier, we were struck by terrible winds, and we thought we had lost one of the brigs. The storm brought us to this city of Cartagena, where we declared before Your Majesty's judge and officials our record of the gold we carried with us, which they melted down and stamped. In Your Majesty's best interest, they provided us with the necessary provisions and equipment to continue our journey. And from here, on the eighth day of July we will depart together in a ship that at present is in this port and is bound for the kingdoms of Spain.[29] May it please our Lord God that Your Majesty's victories continue in perpetuity, adding many more kingdoms and dominions, and spreading our holy Catholic faith.

S.C.C.M.[30]
Servants and subjects of Your Majesty who kiss your royal hands and feet.

Signed Juan de San Martín and Antonio de Lebrija.

---

29. On the same day, Cartagena's governor and *juez de residencia,* Juan de Santa Cruz, wrote a letter to the Crown, surely with the intention of sending it to Spain with Jiménez de Quesada. In the letter, Santa Cruz writes that Jiménez and the others had arrived in Cartagena more than three weeks earlier, on June 21. See Carta de Juan de Santa Cruz, AGI Santo Domingo 49, N. 65, R. 10, fols. 1r–2v.

30. Sacra Cesarea Católica Magestad.

*Excerpt from the "Epítome de la conquista
del Nuevo Reino de Granada," fol. 7*

Unlike the previous excerpt from Juan de San Martín and Antonio
de Lebrija's letter, the final folio of the "Epítome de la conquista
del Nuevo Reino de Granada" offers few details of the conquest
of Muisca territory. There is no mention of the sacking of Tunja,
the distribution of the booty, the alliance with Sagipa against the
Panches, or Sagipa's subsequent capture, torture, and death. Instead,
the last page of the Epítome highlights the arrival of the Nicolás
Federmán and Sebastián Belalcázar expeditions in early 1539, and
Jiménez's decision to return to Spain. The account ends with a brief
mention of the legal disputes between Jiménez and don Alonso Luis
de Lugo over the rights to New Granada, as well as the rewards and
honors granted to Jiménez for his services to the Crown.

In addition to his lengthy disputes with don Alonso Luis de Lugo,
Jiménez also faced a series of charges when he returned to Spain,
including fraud, torture, and murder. Several veterans of the expedition filed suits against the *licenciado,* claiming that they had been
promised shares in the spoils. Jiménez successfully defended himself
against most charges, but he did have a pay a series of fines, and he
was forbidden to return to the lands he had conquered. In fact, only
in 1548 was Jiménez granted license to return to the New Kingdom
of Granada.

Returning to matters of this New Kingdom, I say that most of the
year 1538 was spent completing the subjugation and pacification of
the kingdom. Once that was accomplished, *licenciado* Jiménez recognized the need to colonize the kingdom with Spaniards; with that in
mind, he built three illustrious cities. One of these is in the province
of Bogotá; he named it Santa Fe. The other was given the name Tunja,
the same name as the land in which it is located. And he called the
other Vélez, which is located next to where Jiménez and his men had
[first] entered this kingdom. It already was 1539 when all of that
was completed. With that done, *licenciado* Jiménez decided to return
to Spain to give your Majesty a personal account, and to negotiate
his affairs in person. He left his brother, Hernán Pérez de Quesada,
behind as his lieutenant. In preparation for his journey, Jiménez

ordered that new brigs be built beside the Río Grande; he wanted to find a different route to the river from the New Kingdom, which they found on the other side of Panche territory, roughly twenty-five leagues from the New Kingdom. Thus, it was unnecessary to cross again over the Opón mountains, from where they had first entered, which would have been extremely difficult.

One month before licenciado Jiménez departed for Spain, Nicolás Federmán, on behalf of the Germans, came to the New Kingdom from the direction of Venezuela; Federmán's Indian translators had informed him that he was approaching a very rich land. Federmán served as captain and lieutenant to Jorge Espira, governor of the province of Venezuela, and he brought with him one hundred and fifty soldiers. Within fifteen days of Federmán's arrival, Sebastián de Benalcázar, captain and lieutenant of Quito, on authority from the Marqués don Francisco Pizarro, arrived from the other direction; he also brought with him more than one hundred soldiers. Benalcázar, like Federmán, had been lured to [the New Kingdom] by tales of fabulous riches. However, both captains were greatly disappointed to learn that they had been outwitted, and that *licenciado* Jiménez and the people from Santa Marta already had been in the region for almost three years. Nevertheless, *licenciado* Jiménez accepted the newcomers because he needed people to distribute among the Spanish towns that he had built. He took in all of Federmán's men, and half of Benalcázar's; the other half he sent back to a province called Popayán, located between Quito and the New Kingdom, which Benalcázar had settled, and at present serves as governor. After taking the two captains' men and assigning them to the various cities, Jiménez ordered that Federmán and Benalcázar accompany him for the coast, and then to Spain. However, both captains were greatly irritated by this, as well as the seizure of their men. In particular, Nicolás Federmán complained that Jiménez had committed a flagrant injustice by not returning his men and granting him the freedom to return to Venezuela. In spite of this, Jiménez removed both Benalcázar and Federmán from the region and brought them in the brigantines to the coast. From there, they were delighted to return to Spain. *Licenciado* Jiménez arrived in Spain in November of '39,[31] precisely at the

---

31. According to Gil López, who traveled back to Spain with Jiménez de Quesada, a storm forced their ship to dock at Málaga, where they arrived safely on November 14, 1539. See AGI Escribanía 1006A, Cuaderno 3, fol. 114r.

time when Your Majesty was beginning to cross through France on the way to Flanders.

Licenciado Jiménez brought several lawsuits against the *adelantado* of the Canary Islands, don Alonso de Lugo. Lugo is married to doña Beatríz de Noroña, who is the sister of doña María de Mendoza, wife of León's *comendador mayor*. The legal proceedings were all related to this New Kingdom of Granada, because don Alonso claimed that his father, [don Pedro Fernández de Lugo] had been granted the governorship of Santa Marta for two lives, one for the father and one for the son, and that the New Kingdom fell within the demarcation of the province of Santa Marta. Therefore, the members of the Council of the Indies ordered that Lugo return to Santa Marta;[32] and they placed the administration of the New Kingdom under the authority of Santa Marta, and don Alonso went there to govern them. He later returned to Spain, and in order to better govern the New Kingdom, Your Majesty has placed a royal chancery there, with several judges who are in charge of both that province and neighboring ones.

Licenciado Jiménez named this region the New Kingdom of Granada for two reasons. In Spain Jiménez resided in the Kingdom of Granada, and the two Granadas look very much alike; both are situated among hills and mountains, both have climates that are colder than they are hot, and they differ little in size. For having discovered, won, and settled this kingdom in your service, Your Majesty rewarded Jiménez with the title of *mariscal* of the said kingdom, with an annual salary of two thousand *ducados*, paid in perpetuity from the royal treasury of this kingdom, for Jiménez and for his descendents. Furthermore, to compensate for his absence from the New Kingdom, Your Majesty added a provision that Jiménez be given Indians [in *encomienda*], with an annual tribute of more than eight thousand *ducados*. Your Majesty also named him *alcalde* of the kingdom's principal city, with a corresponding annual salary of four hundred *ducados*; and Jiménez also was awarded certain offices, and other things of lesser value. *Licenciado* Gonzalo Jiménez de Quesada,

32. This matter was finally resolved with the promulgation of a royal decree dated November 22, 1538; acting on the final recommendation of the Council of the Indies, King Charles V decreed that the terms of the 1536 *capitulación* (including the governorship of Santa Marta) with don Pedro Fernández de Lugo be transferred to don Alonso. Two years later the Crown issued another decree ordering Lugo to return to Santa Marta to assume his governorship. See Avellaneda Navas, *Expedición de Alonso Luis de Lugo*, 12.

the current *mariscal* of the New Kingdom of Granada, is the son of the Licenciado Gonzalo Jiménez and his wife Isabel de Quesada. They reside in the *mariscal's* native city of Granada; Jiménez's ancestors hail from the city of Córdoba.

Excerpt from the Anonymous "Relación de Santa Marta"
(c. 1545), AGI Patronato 27, R. 9, fols. 13v–16r

The following excerpt from the anonymous "Relación de Santa Marta" chronicles many of the same events described above in San Martín and Lebrija's letter. However, there are some striking differences between the two accounts. For one thing, the Relación offers a slightly different chronology of events, with the expedition to Neiva taking place before the attack on Bogotá's mountain retreat. The account below continues the Relación from the excerpt in Chapter 4.

It is interesting to note that the anonymous Relación offers a distinct perspective on the circumstances of Bogotá's death and the story of Sagipa. According to the San Martín and Lebrija version of the surprise attack on Bogotá's mountain retreat, the Bogotá had attempted to escape by dressing in ragged clothing, only to be killed by some Spaniards who did not know his true identity. By contrast, the author of the Relación claims that four Spaniards (two horsemen and two foot soldiers) secretly murdered the *cacique* in order to steal the rich robes that adorned his body. Both accounts reveal few details about the circumstances of Sagipa's torture and death, but they give very different accounts of Sagipa's claim to the title of Bogotá. San Martín and Lebrija identify Sagipa as the previous Bogotá's nephew and consequently the legitimate heir to the office, whereas the author of the Relación identifies Sagipa as nothing more than a war captain who usurped the title of Bogotá by force.

From the emerald mines, Captain Valenzuela returned to camp, bringing with him three or four valuable stones that the Indians had presented him. The camp was located at Turmequé, and while there, Jiménez sent some captains, led by Captain Cardoso, to launch an assault. They captured a number of Indians, two of whom promised Cardoso that they would take him to the great *cacique* Tunja. They claimed that Tunja possessed three houses filled with gold, and that the support posts on the houses were all made of gold. Therefore, the

Christians decided to go there. The Indian guides led them through many towns, and a journey that should have taken no more than one day turned into a fourteen-day expedition. When they approached Tunja, they marched forward at great speed. At sunset, they arrived to where the lord Tunja lived, and they took the *cacique* captive. The lieutenant Jiménez dismounted, followed by Captain Céspedes and several other captains. Captain Cardoso remained on horseback, apprehensive of all the people they saw gathering. Those who had dismounted from their horses rushed the *cacique*, and all the gold and emerald stones they found, out of harm's way. In the meantime, Captain Cardoso and his men patrolled around the lord Tunja's fenced houses. It took until the early hours of the morning to gather all the gold, emerald stones, beads, and fine *mantas*. The Christians seized a great quantity of everything, especially clothing, which was of very fine quality. During the entire night, they heard great murmurs and mutterings that the Indians were about to riot. A scuffle ensued shortly before daybreak, and some Indian allies perished while defending lord Tunja and Captain Cardoso. Exhausted, and frightened by the sight of the Indians they had killed, the Spaniards stopped fighting. Captain Cardoso dismounted, and placed guards on sentry duty in order to prevent the Indians from attacking again.

That night the Christians seized close to 180,000 pesos of fine and low-grade gold, as well as a great number of emeralds. The sun had not been up for three hours when another group of Indians attacked; however, having placed sentries on duty, and being well rested from the night before, the Christians quickly mounted their horses and rode against the Indians, forcing their retreat. With the fighting ended, the Christians began to negotiate with the *cacique* Tunja, informing him that they had heard reports that he possessed a great quantity of gold. And the Christians promised that they would release him and be his friend and ally if the *cacique* gave them the gold. Tunja promised to deliver it, but he brought only false promises. At times he would say that certain Indians had taken the gold and had hidden it in the mountains. At other times, he claimed that he had buried it himself, making the Christians dig holes around many of his residences; but they never found a thing.

Seeing this, the Christians decided to move against another *cacique*, who resided eight or nine leagues away from Tunja. His name was Sogamoso, and it was rumored that he possessed a great quantity of gold. However, Sogamoso did not await their arrival and instead fled. In Sogamoso's sanctuaries, the Christians discovered upward of thirty thousand pesos of gold in precious objects, fashioned in the shapes of eagles and crowns, which Sogamoso had offered to his *tunxos*, or gods. They found other jewels of various kinds, gold *texuelos*, and some gold leaf worth about ten marks. And they found some emeralds, some beads, and some fine *mantas*. At a nearby mountain, they had a brief skirmish with some Indians. From there the Christians returned to Tunja, where they remained for several days. While in Tunja, a neighboring *cacique,* himself a great lord and valiant warrior, sent some of his Indians to warn the Christians that he intended to kill them all, and make shields from the skins of their horses, and use their teeth to make necklaces for his women. And when the Christians least expected it, a large number of his Indians launched a surprise attack. A battle ensued, and the Indians were routed; a great number of Indians died there.

For weapons, the Indians carried very strong palm spears, some thirty and thirty-five hands in length. And they wielded *macanas,* which are like swords. They also used arrows from the same palm, and some carried shields. With great order and discipline they arrived and waited in the open battlefield; but they all fled at the first sight of the carnage inflicted upon them by the Christians.

Several days after the battle occurred, and in order to convince the Christians to leave their territory, the Indians told stories of a land called Neiva, located toward Quito, in which there was a great quantity of gold. The Indians spoke of a house that was filled with gold trinkets, and the same house had support posts made entirely from gold. The reports filled the Christians with a great desire to go there. Jiménez thus appointed Captain San Martín, Captain Céspedes, Captain Cardoso, Captain Lebrija, Captain Albarrazín, Captain Suárez, and several other Spaniards to accompany him to Neiva.

Jiménez left his brother Hernán Pérez de Quesada, as well as Captain Juan del Junco, in charge to guard the camp and all the gold, and he departed with the above-mentioned people toward Neiva. They arrived in the land of Bogotá and from there they made their way to the town of Pasca. There, the Indians from Pasca showed them which path to take, which they knew well because they carry salt to Neiva, which they exchange for gold. The Christians also learned in Pasca that the road to Neiva crossed through vast, uninhabited lands, and that there would be no place to procure foodstuffs except for one small village, which stored nothing but potatoes. Therefore, the Christians gathered their provisions in Pasca, with supplies of bread, dried meat, and maize; they also brought four hundred Indian men and women carriers, each loaded with food and provisions. They endured many hardships on this expedition. At long last they arrived in Neiva, where they found absolutely nothing of which the Indians had spoken. Instead, they found that they were back beside the Río Grande; on the other side of the bank they saw a settlement of reasonable size, and they began to engage the Indians in conversation. They spoke at great length, until at last an Indian leader came across the river. He brought with him some gold patens, which were probably worth 300 or 400 pesos. The Indian claimed that he had no more gold; and the Christians were unable to convince him to give them more, until they threatened to cross over to the other side unless [the Indians] brought more gold and made peace. On hearing this, the Indian returned with more gold, but it was very little. Lieutenant Jiménez therefore decided to send Captain Cardoso and some of his men across to the other bank; however, because the river was so wide and so violent, none of the men chosen for the task dared to cross. Thus, they all returned to camp. Later, eight or ten men dared to undertake the crossing with Captain Cardoso. And they made it across, with three horses; all the other horses returned because of the strong current. When the Indians saw that they had made it across, they all took flight, leaving the town completely abandoned. Cardoso and the others searched the entire settlement. They found no gold, except in one house where they came across some dead bodies, wrapped in *mantas*. On these mantas, just above the chests, the Indians had fastened some large sheets of very fine gold, in the shape of the moon. They could be worth up to one thousand *ducados*, and thus Captain Cardoso returned from across the river.

With Cardoso and the others returned, the Christians decided to send Captain San Martín and Captain Céspedes to explore upriver. Lieutenant Jiménez remained behind with the others. The two captains were gone for eight or ten days, at which point they returned to camp for lack of iron fittings for their horses. Because the land is extremely rocky, horseshoes wear quickly, and it took them no time at all before they had no horseshoes left. Furthermore, this land is very unhealthy; in the little time that the Christians roamed around in its heat, not a single man remained who had not fallen ill. One soldier died, and many others would have if they had lingered any longer. Thus, they all returned to Bogotá, and from there they journeyed to Tunja, where they remained for several days, trying to make peace with the local *caciques*. From there, the entire camp returned to Bogotá, where they began to establish friendships with certain *caciques*.

The *cacique* Suba Usaque[33] came to the Christians as a great friend and ally, and his loyalty never wavered. The reason for this friendship was: Suba Usaque's son-in-law, the *cacique* Bogotá, learned that Suba Usaque earlier had gone to see the Christians and had given them food and other things. And because Bogotá was a more powerful lord [than his father-in-law], he had Suba Usaque arrested, many of his houses burned, and large numbers of his Indians executed. He also stole some of his gold. For that reason, Suba Usaque later became a close ally to the Christians, and he has remained a loyal friend.

With matters thus, the Christians learned where Bogotá was hiding, which was high in a mountain where the *cacique* had built some houses, protected by surrounding walls. The Christians decided one night to go out to capture him. They left the camp where it was, and they approached to within three leagues of Bogotá's location. From there, the Christians dispatched messengers in order to assure Bogotá that they did not want to wage war against him; rather, they wanted to make peace. And they requested that the *cacique* issue a response by the following day because they could wait no longer. Bogotá sent neither messenger nor message of any kind. Thus, on the following day, the Christians seized all of the Indian men and women who served Bogotá. They left these Indians in their lodgings, with their hands and feet tied. There they remained until past nightfall, tightly bound so that none of them could escape to warn Bogotá, or anyone else for that matter. The Christians departed at 10:00 in the evening, silently, so as not to be heard. One or two hours before sunrise they arrived at Bogotá's enclosure. There they placed soldiers and horsemen around the outside walls so that no one could escape without

33. Like so many other Chibcha words, the precise meaning of the term *usaque* remains unclear. It appears to have been an honorific title held by a small number of powerful leaders, perhaps military men, whose rank fell somewhere between the *zipa* (supreme political ruler) and the local *cacique* (chief). See Kurella, "Muisca," 196; and Gamboa, "Caciques muiscas," 62.

being captured. Lieutenant Jiménez and many others rushed inside and seized some Indians. Many others escaped. It was learned later that Bogotá managed to flee through a trap door. As fortune would have it, two horsemen and two foot soldiers happened to be guarding Bogotá's escape route. In their great lust to steal the rich *manta* that Bogotá was wearing, the soldiers stabbed the *cacique* with a knife. And after taking his *manta*, they let the injured Bogotá go free; later, the soldiers falsely claimed that not a single Indian had passed through the area where they had stood guard.

And that was how the *cacique* was injured, there on the mountain, very close to where he died. No one knew until his body was discovered by some birds, called *gallinas*,[34] which eat human flesh. The Indians watched as those birds gathered in that place to feast; and because they could not locate Bogotá, they followed the birds, suspecting what they would find. There they discovered his corpse. However, the Christians did not learn of his death for another year, and they thought he was still alive.

From there, the Christians returned to where they had left the Indians bound, but they had all escaped, having been untied by other Indians from the area. From there, they sent a message back to camp to have the others join them. After several months, they learned of Bogotá's death. They also discovered that one of Bogotá's great captains, called Sagipa, had risen up and usurped control of the land. With all kinds of flattery and affection, the Christians endeavored to lure Sagipa to come forward and make peace; and after a few months he came to them. He told them that he was at war with the Panches, a fierce people who eat human flesh, and he requested Jiménez's assistance to go to Panche territory to kill them. If the Christians agreed to help, then he would be their friend, and he would accompany them. Lieutenant Jiménez accepted, and the Christians joined Sagipa. Together, they engaged the Panches in battle and killed many of them. They all then returned to where they had camped. Sagipa proceeded to flee from the Christians, moving stealthily about the region. The Christians therefore decided to take matters into their own hands and they had Sagipa arrested. They marched over to where he was, and, somewhat against his will, they brought the *cacique* back to camp. On his arrival, Lieutenant Jiménez spoke to him

34. The birds were probably turkey buzzards.

on behalf of the entire camp, telling him that Bogotá was an enemy of the Christians, and as their enemy he had died. Therefore, all of Bogotá's gold, as it was enemy property, belonged to the king and to the Christians. Jiménez ordered Sagipa to hand the gold over, because they knew for certain that he had it. The lieutenant added that he was not asking Sagipa to relinquish any of his own possessions; instead, the Christians only wanted what had belonged to Bogotá. Sagipa responded that he would, with great pleasure, give them the gold. He asked them to extend him a reasonable deadline in order to do so, promising that he would fill a small house with Bogotá's gold; but he needed a few days in order to gather all the gold. They granted the time that Sagipa had requested; and they kept him under guard in order to prevent him from escaping. During that time, Indian messengers came and went, but when the deadline expired Sagipa had not complied. He handed over three or four thousand pesos of fine and low-grade gold, and nothing more. Seeing this, the Christians began to plead with Lieutenant Jiménez to place Sagipa in irons and have him tortured. The lieutenant chose not do that, which sparked many grumblings that Jiménez had reached some accord with the *cacique*. Thus, the Christians all came together and renewed their pleas, granting legal authority to Jerónimo de Ayusa[35] to argue their case. Seeing this, Jiménez appointed his brother, Hernán Pérez de Quesada, who was administered the oath as Sagipa's defender. Both Ayusa and Pérez de Quesada argued their cases as best they possibly could, after which point the Christians proceeded to torture Sagipa in order to compel him to hand over Bogotá's gold and confess where he had hidden it; in the end, Sagipa died.[36]

35. Jerónimo de Ayusa's last name is sometimes written as Inza.

36. The "Relación de Santa Marta" does not end here. The anonymous account contains another four pages, in which the author discusses briefly the arrival of the expeditions led by Sebastián de Belalcázar from Quito and Nicolás de Federmán from Venezuela. It then discusses how Jiménez assigned *encomienda* grants before he, Belalcázar, and Federmán all returned to Cartagena and then to Spain in order to present their claims over the new territory before the Crown. There is also a brief account of Hernán Pérez de Quesada's tenure as lieutenant, his campaigns against the Panches, and his quest to find the Casa del Sol (House of the Sun) and El Dorado. And there is an account of Jerónimo Lebrón's arrival in Santa Marta as the new governor, as well as his 1539 expedition to the New Kingdom. The Relación ends with Lebrón's departure from Santa Marta in 1540 and the arrival of the new governor, the *adelantado* Alonso Luis de Lugo. The last sentence of the account refers to the year 1545, when Lugo departed once again for Spain. For a complete transcription of the "Relación de Santa Marta," see Tovar Pinzón, *Relaciones y visitas a los Andes*, 2:125–88.

BIBLIOGRAPHY

Primary Archival Sources

AGI   Archivo General de Indias, Seville, Spain

Published Sources

Aguado, Friar Pedro. *Recopilación historial.* 4 vols. Bogotá: Empresa Nacional de Publicaciones, 1956–57.

Aguilar Rodas, Raúl. *Pedro de Cieza de León y la historia de Colombia.* Santafé de Bogotá, 2000.

Arciniegas, Germán. *Jiménez de Quesada.* Bogota: ABC, 1939.

———. *The Knight of El Dorado: The Tale of Don Gonzalo Jiménez de Quesada and His Conquest of New Granada, Now Called Colombia.* Translated by Mildred Adams. New York: Viking Press, 1968.

Ariza, Alberto. "Itinerario cronológico y geográfico de la expedición de Jiménez de Quesada al reino Chibcha." *Boletín Cultural y Bibliográfico* 6, no. 7 (1963): 984–87.

Avellaneda Navas, José Ignacio. *Los compañeros de Féderman, cofundadores de Santa Fe de Bogotá.* Bogotá: Tercer Mundo Editores, 1990.

———. *The Conquerors of the New Kingdom of Granada.* Albuquerque: University of New Mexico Press, 1995.

———. *La expedición de Alonso Luis de Lugo al Nuevo Reino de Granada.* Bogotá: Banco de la República, 1994.

———. *La expedición de Gonzalo Jiménez de Quesada al Mar del Sur y la creación del Nuevo Reino de Granada.* Bogotá: Banco de la República, 1995.

———. *La expedición de Sebastián de Belalcázar al Mar del Norte y su llegada al Nuevo Reino de Granada.* Bogotá: Banco de la República, 1992.

———. *La jornada de Jerónimo Lebrón al Nuevo Reino de Granada.* Bogotá: Banco de la República, 1993.

Ballesteros, Manuel. *Gonzalo Jiménez de Quesada.* Madrid: Quorum, 1987.

Broadbent, Sylvia M. *Los Chibchas: Organización socio-político.* Bogotá: Imprenta Nacional, 1964.

———. "The Formation of Peasant Society in Central Colombia." *Ethnohistory* 28, no. 3 (1981): 259–77.

Brown, Kendall. "Alcabala." In *Iberia and the Americas: Culture, Politics, and History,* ed. J. Michael Francis, 3 vols., 1:57–58. Santa Barbara, Calif.: ABC-Clio, 2006.

Burkholder, Mark A., and Lyman L. Johnson. *Colonial Latin America.* 5th ed. New York: Oxford University Press, 1994.

Bushnell, David. *The Making of Modern Colombia: A Nation in Spite of Itself.* Berkeley and Los Angeles: University of California Press, 1993.

Castellanos, Juan. *Elegías de varones ilustres de Indias.* 1586. Bogotá: Gerardo Rivas Moreno, 1997.

Cieza de León, Pedro de. *The Discovery and Conquest of Peru.* Edited and translated by Alexandra Parma Cook and Noble David Cook. Durham: Duke University Press, 1998.

Cline, Howard. "The *Relaciones Geográficas* of the Spanish Indies, 1577–1586." *Hispanic American Historical Review* 44, no. 3 (1964): 341–74.

Colmenares, Germán. *La provincia de Tunja en el Nuevo Reino de Granada.* Bogotá: Universidad de los Andes, 1970.

Conway, Richard. "Caciques." In *Iberia and the Americas: Culture, Politics, and History,* ed. J. Michael Francis, 3 vols., 1:167–69. Santa Barbara, Calif.: ABC-Clio, 2006.

Fernández Armesto, Felipe. *The Canary Islands After the Conquest: The Making of a Colonial Society in the Early Sixteenth Century.* Oxford: Clarendon Press, 1982.

Fernández Piedrahita, Lucas. *Historia general de las conquistas del Nuevo Reino de Granada.* 1688. Bogotá: Editorial ABC, 1942.

Francis, J. Michael, ed. *Iberia and the Americas: Culture, Politics, and History.* 3 vols. Santa Barbara, Calif.: ABC-Clio, 2006.

———. "'In the service of God, I order that these temples of idolatrous worship be razed to the ground': Extirpation of Idolatry and the Search for the *Santuario Grande* of Iguaque." In *Colonial Lives: Documents on Latin American History, 1550–1850,* ed. Richard Boyer and Geoffrey Spurling, 39–53. Oxford: Oxford University Press, 2000.

———. "Población, enfermedad y cambio demográfico, 1537–1636: Demografía histórica de Tunja-Una mirada crítica." *Fronteras de la Historia* 7 (2002): 15–95.

———. "The *Resguardo,* the *Mita,* and the *Alquiler General:* Indian Migration in the Province of Tunja, 1550–1636." *Colonial Latin American Historical Review* 11, no. 4 (2002): 375–406.

Friede, Juan. *El adelantado Don Gonzalo Jiménez de Quesada.* 2 vols. Bogotá: Carlos Valencia Editores, 1979.

———. "Antecedentes histórico-geográficos del descubrimiento de la meseta Chibcha por el licenciado Jiménez de Quesada." *Revista de Indias* 10, no. 40 (1950): 327–48.

———. *Descubrimiento del Nuevo Reino de Granada y fundación de Bogotá.* Bogotá: Banco de la República, 1960.

———, ed. *Documentos inéditos para la historia de Colombia [1509–1550].* 10 vols. Bogotá: Academia Colombiana de la Historia, 1955–60.

———. *Gonzalo Jiménez de Quesada a través de documentos históricos.* Bogotá: ABC, 1960.

———. *Invasión del país de los Chibchas: Conquista del Nuevo Reino de Granada y fundación de Bogotá.* Bogotá: Tercer Mundo, 1966.

Gálvis, Madero, Luis. *El adelantado.* Madrid: Ediciones Guadarrama, S.L., 1957.

Gamboa M., Jorge Augusto. "Los caciques muiscas y la transición al regimen colonial en el altiplano cundiboyacense durante el siglo XVI (1537–1560)." In *Muiscas: Representaciones, cartografías, y etnopolíticas de la memoria,* ed. Ana María Gómez Londoño, 54–72. Bogotá: Editorial Pontificia Universidad Javeriana, 2005.

———. "Los Muisca y la conquista española: Nuevas interpretaciones de un viejo problema." Paper, 2006.

Gómez Londoño, Ana María, ed. *Muiscas: Representaciones, cartografías, y etnopolíticas de la memoria.* Bogotá: Editorial Pontificia Universidad Javeriana, 2005.

Gómez Pérez, María del Carmen. *Pedro de Heredia y Cartagena de Indias.* Seville: Escuela de Estudios Hispano-Americanos, 1984.

González de Pérez, María Stella. *Diccionario y gramática Chibcha: Manuscrito anónimo de la Biblioteca Nacional de Colombia.* Bogotá: Instituto Caro y Cuervo, 1987.

Graham, R. B. Cunninghame. *The Conquest of New Granada: Being the Life of Gonzalo Jiménez de Quesada.* Boston: Houghton Mifflin, 1922.

Haring, Clarence Henry. *The Spanish Empire in America.* New York: Oxford University Press, 1947.

———. *Trade and Navigation Between Spain and the Indies in the Time of the Hapsburgs.* Cambridge: Harvard University Press, 1918.

Hassig, Ross. *Mexico and the Spanish Conquest.* 2d ed. Norman: University of Oklahoma Press, 2006.

Hemming, John. *The Conquest of the Incas.* London: Macmillan, 1970.

———. *The Search for El Dorado.* London: Phoenix Press, 1978.

Kroeber, A. L. "The Chibcha." In *Handbook of South American Indians,* ed. Julian H. Steward, 12 vols., vol. 2, *The Andrean Civilizations,* 887–909. New York: Cooper Square Publishers, 1963.

Kurella, Doris. "The Muisca: Chiefdoms in Transition." In *Chiefdoms and Chieftaincy in the Americas,* ed. Elsa M. Redmond, 189–216. Gainesville: University Press of Florida, 1998.

Langebaek, Carl Henrik. *Mercados, poblamientos e integración étnica entre los muiscas: Siglo XVI.* Bogotá: Banco de la República, 1987.

Lockhart, James. *The Men of Cajamarca: A Social and Biographical Study of the First Conquerors of Peru.* Austin: University of Texas Press, 1972.

———. *We People Here: Nahuatl Accounts of the Conquest of Mexico.* Berkeley and Los Angeles: University of California Press, 2000.

MacLeod, Murdo J. "Self-Promotion: The Relaciones de Méritos y Servicios and Their Historical and Political Interpretation." *Colonial Latin American Historical Review* 7, no. 1 (1998): 25–42.

Markham, Sir Clements. *The Conquest of New Granada*. Port Washington, N.Y.: Kennikat Press, 1912.

McFarlane, Anthony. *Colombia Before Independence: Economy, Society, and Politics Under Bourbon Rule*. Cambridge: Cambridge University Press, 1993.

Migarro Arnandis, Mariángeles. *Tributo y familia en Nueva Granada: La provincia de Tunja en los siglos XVII y XVIII*. Castelló de la Plana: Universitat Jaume I, 2004.

Millán de Benavides, Carmen. *Epítome de la conquista del Nuevo Reino de Granada: La cosmografía española del siglo XVI y el conocimiento por cuestionario*. Bogotá: CEJA, 2001.

Oviedo y Valdés, Gonzalo Fernández de. *Historia general y natural de las Indias*. 5 vols. Edited by Juan Pérez de Tudela Bueso. Madrid: Atlas, 1959.

Pike, Ruth. *Aristocrats and Traders: Sevillian Society in the Sixteenth Century*. Ithaca: Cornell University Press, 1972.

Ramos Pérez, Demetrio. *Ximenez de Quesada en su relación con los cronistas y el epítome de la conquista del Nuevo Reino de Granada*. Seville: Escuela de Estudios Hispano-Americanos, 1972.

Restall, Matthew. "Cabildo." In *Iberia and the Americas: Culture, Politics and History*, ed. J. Michael Francis, 3 vols., 1:165–66. Santa Barbara, Calif.: ABC-Clio, 2006.

———. *Seven Myths of the Spanish Conquest*. New York: Oxford University Press, 2003.

Restall, Matthew, Lisa Sousa, and Kevin Terraciano, eds. *Mesoamerican Voices: Native Writings from Colonial Mexico, Oaxaca, Yucatan, and Guatemala*. Cambridge: Cambridge University Press, 2005.

Restrepo Tirado, Ernesto. *Historia de la provincia de Santa Marta*. Seville: Imprenta y Librerería de Eugelio de las Heras, 1929.

Rodríguez Freyle, Juan. *Conquista y descubrimiento del Nuevo Reino de Granada*. Edited by Jaime Delgado. Madrid: Historia 16, 1986.

Rosa, Moisés de la. "Los Conquistadores de los Chibchas." *Boletín de Historia y Antigüedades* 22 (1935): 225–53.

Rosa Olivera, Leopoldo de la. "Don Pedro Fernández de Lugo prepara la expedición a Santa Marta." *Anuario de Estudios Atlánticos* 5 (1959): 399–444.

Safford, Frank, and Marco Palacios. *Colombia: Fragmented Land, Divided Society*. New York: Oxford University Press, 2002.

Schwartz, Stuart B., ed. *Victors and Vanquished: Spanish and Nahua Views of the Conquest of Mexico*. Boston: Bedford/St. Martin's, 2000.

Simón, Friar Pedro. *Noticias historiales de las conquistas de tierra firme en las Indias Occidentales*. 7 vols. Bogotá: Banco Popular Español, 1981–82.

Thomas, Hugh. *Conquest: Montezuma, Cortés, and the Fall of Old Mexico*. New York: Simon and Schuster, 1993.

———. *Rivers of Gold: The Rise of the Spanish Empire from Columbus to Magellan.* New York: Random House, 2003.

Tovar Pinzón, Hermes. *La formación social Chibcha.* Bogotá: Universidad Nacional de Colombia, 1980.

———. *No hay caciques ni señores.* Barcelona: Sendai, D.L., 1988.

———. *Relaciones y visitas a los Andes: S. XVI.* Vol. 2, *Región del Caribe;* vol. 3, *Región Central-Oriental.* Bogotá: Colcultura, 1993.

Villamarín, Juan. "*Encomenderos* and Indians in the Formation of Colonial Society in the Sabana de Bogotá, 1537–1740." Ph.D. diss., Brandeis University, 1972.

Villamarín, Juan, and Judith Villamarín. "Chiefdoms: The Prevalence and Persistence of "Señorías Naturales": 1400 to European Conquest." In *The Cambridge History of Native Peoples of the Americas,* vol. 3, *South America,* ed. Frank Salomon and Stuart B. Schwartz, 577–656. Cambridge: Cambridge University Press, 1999.

latin american originals

Series Editor | Matthew Restall

This series features primary source texts on colonial and nineteenth-century Latin America, translated into English, in slim, accessible, affordable editions that also make scholarly contributions. Most of these sources are being published in English for the first time and represent an alternative to the traditional texts on early Latin America. The initial focus is on the conquest period in sixteenth-century Spanish America, but subsequent volumes include Brazil, as well as later centuries. The series features archival documents and printed sources originally in Spanish, Portuguese, Latin, and various Native American languages. The contributing authors are historians, anthropologists, art historians, and scholars of literature.

Matthew Restall is Edwin Erle Sparks Professor of Latin American History and Anthropology, and Director of Latin American Studies, at the Pennsylvania State University. He is co-editor of the journal Ethnohistory. J. Michael Francis is Associate Professor of Latin American History at the University of North Florida.

Associate Series Editor | J. Michael Francis

Board of Editorial Consultants

Noble David Cook | Edward F. Fischer | Susan Kellogg
Elizabeth W. Kiddy | Kris E. Lane | Alida C. Metcalf
Susan Schroeder | John F. Schwaller | Ben Vinson III

Titles in print

Invading Colombia: Spanish Accounts of the
Gonzalo Jiménez de Quesada Expedition of Conquest (LAO 1)
J. Michael Francis

Invading Guatemala: Spanish, Nahua,
and Maya Accounts of the Conquest Wars (LAO 2)
Matthew Restall and Florine Asselbergs